On the Way

Vocation, Awareness,
and Fly Fishing

Presbyterian Church
of Chestertown

On the Way

Vocation, Awareness, and Fly Fishing

Kenneth Arnold

A
JourneyBook ™
from
Church Publishing Incorporated New York

Cover photograph of the Philosopher's Path, Kyoto, Japan, by Kenneth Arnold.

Some of the essays in this book were originally published
in somewhat different form in
Episcopal Life, The Open Circle, and Faith@Work.

Library of Congress Cataloging-in-Publication Data

Arnold, Kenneth.
On the way : vocation, awareness, and fly fishing / Kenneth Arnold.
        p. cm. – (JourneyBook)
"Some of the essays in this book were originally published in somewhat different
    form in Episcopal Life, the Open Circle, and Faith @ Work."
        ISBN 0-89869-337-3 (pbk.)
        1. Meditations. 2. Arnold, Kenneth, I. Title.

BV4832.2 .A734 2000
283'.092—dc21
[B]

                                                            00-060332

JourneyBook and colophon are registered trademarks of Church Publishing Incorporated

Church Publishing Incorporated
445 Fifth Avenue
New York, NY 10016

http://www.churchpublishing.org

5 4 3 2 1

For Ken Burton, my brother on the way

They came to Jericho. As he and his disciples and a large crowd were leaving Jericho, Bartimaeus son of Timaeus, a blind beggar, was sitting by the roadside. When he heard that it was Jesus of Nazareth, he began to shout out and say, "Jesus, Son of David, have mercy on me!" Many sternly ordered him to be quiet, but he cried out even more loudly, "Son of David, have mercy on me!" Jesus stood still and said, "Call him here." And they called the blind man, saying to him, "Take heart; get up, he is calling you." So throwing off his cloak, he sprang up and came to Jesus. Then Jesus said to him, "What do you want me to do for you?" The blind man said to him, "My teacher, let me see again." Jesus said to him, "Go; your faith has made you well." Immediately he regained his sight and followed him on the way.

Mark 10:45–52

Introduction

ON LEARNING that I was a playwright, a young woman still in college (one of my wife's students), sweetly asked me twenty years ago if I would write a play for the children of St. Mark's Episcopal Church in Philadelphia, where she taught Sunday school.

"Only if I don't have to do dogma and no one wears bathrobes or cotton beards."

I think I agreed because during my senior year in high school I had a brief but intense love affair with the Episcopal Church sweetened by my infatuation with a beautiful Latvian whose family was Episcopalian. The memory of kneeling with her at Morning Prayer still seems a portent of heaven.

Although as an adolescent I expected to be ordained in the Disciples of Christ Church in which I grew up, I precipitously dropped out of church in 1964, while I was in college. I graduated with a degree in English literature and theater, studied creative writing (poetry and plays), and entered a lifelong career in publishing. I did not return to the Church until 1979, when God tricked me into writing that children's play (about Noah's Ark and in rhymed couplets!) and shoved me down the long road to ordination as a deacon in the Episcopal Church. The instrument of my conversion was, I have come to understand, an angel. She came, changed my life, and disappeared. I do not know where she is today.

I devoured the Church, the sacraments, the scriptures like a starving man, nourishing a change that unfolded through the complex journey that is the subject of this book. The same year of my conversion, I was selected to be a fellow at the Eugene O'Neill Theater Center in Waterford, Connecticut, where I developed *She Also Dances*, my most (only) successful play. In 1980, my wife and I adopted two children. In 1982, I became director of Rutgers University Press. The next year *She Also Dances* premiered in Costa Mesa,

California. And seemingly unrelated to any of that—and more important to the shape of my life—I began to think about ordination. Another sixteen years passed—roughly the same amount of time between my leaving the Church and returning to it—before the Bishop of New York laid hands on my head in the Cathedral Church of St. John the Divine in 1998. By then, I had been fired by Rutgers, divorced, and fallen deeply into debt.

There was a night soon after I lost my job when, at about midnight, I stood by the window of my apartment, twenty-seven floors above the street, and considered suicide. I felt betrayed, alone, helpless. There seemed no way to go but down and out. That is not, however, the way offered me, or anyone, by God. Whatever our circumstances, however grim our condition, there is a way through the world. Our task is to locate and follow it. That sounds simple enough, but it is the surprisingly difficult work of living that shapes our being. The way prepared for me was not through that window; only years of daily spiritual practice, communion with the Church, a deepening awareness that I was being actively led, even as I was suffering, kept me from jumping. The way of struggle is the way given to me. It is the way given to everyone. There is no way out—only a way in.

Our way in the world is enlightened by the Holy Spirit. And so am I. My vocation is to be in the world as a revealer of that Spirit. It is the vocation of all Christians. The deacon's job is to show how that vocation might be lived. The task is to bring who I am to bear on what I do, to make of myself one being in Christ. It is harder than it seems, and especially hard when I insist on doing the work alone. In the moment of suicidal despair, I separated myself from the light of the Spirit by allowing my fear and anger to consume me. And then there was no room in me for anything else, not even God's love.

Some ask if I am going to "go on" now to be a priest, but my vocation is not a stop on the way to something else (or something better). I am fully formed as one who takes up residence in places where the faithful and the faithless regard each other suspiciously. For too

· · · · · ·

many people, the Church is separate—and should be separate—from the world: these spheres should have nothing to say to each other. They speak different languages. Some Christians have gone so far as to call themselves "resident aliens." I think that claiming such an identity is dangerous; it reflects triumphalist selection, as if these Christians were above it all, visitors from another planet who own a superior truth. These are the ones who expect to be raptured. My vocation is to be a messenger, called through an angel to become an angel, one who carries the word of God into the world and the word of the world to the people of God. This witness is important precisely because I am not an alien.

Here is the truth of my life: I am a child of the Holy Spirit, who is always with me. This is an outrageous claim. The world is always offended by such statements. Jesus begins his public ministry by reading in the synagogue from Isaiah: "The Spirit of the Lord is upon me, because he has anointed me to bring good news to the poor" (Luke 4:18). He dies for it. This presence can be fearsome. Rilke writes, "Every angel is terrifying."

In the midnight of my life when I had no hope, I came to think of the Spirit not as a pleasant fluttering dove but as The Beak—a bird that attacks like a plunging hawk, is on us in an instant, snatches us out of our dream lives, and deposits us, often unceremoniously, in God's reality. It is the only way to go.

· · · · · ·

1

· · · · · ·

THE CATHOLIC PRIEST and poet, Ernesto Cardenal, one of the creators of liberation theology, said to me, "You must visit us in our home in Nicaragua." It was the spring of 1973, and we were in a taxi on our way to celebrate the marriage of peace activists Philip and Elizabeth Berrigan at the Cathedral of St. John the Divine. The publisher I worked for, Johns Hopkins, was issuing the first English translation of *Homage to the American Indians*, a book of Ernesto's poems, and we were meeting to discuss details. He had come to New York to raise money for victims of the recent Managua earthquake.

Five years later, Ernesto would become Minister of Culture in the Sandinista government in Nicaragua.

In Cathedral House, a building on the grounds of St. John's, we joined in a Eucharist celebrated by the Jesuit prophet and poet Daniel Berrigan. Seated on the floor of a large room, thirty or forty of us passed around a loaf of bread and drank Almadén wine. It seemed more like a party than a religious service. For a man like me, raised in the Christian Church (Disciples of Christ), it was a shock to my spiritual system (an illicit thrill) to be participating in a Roman Catholic Mass—even a decidedly irregular one—led by the notorious Berrigan, who had just been released from prison. The event showed me a place I had never been—where faith and public life might be celebrated together.

In the fall of 1973, I visited Ernesto's home in the Solentiname archipelago at the southern end of Lake Nicaragua, near Costa Rica. He had established an intentional community there, known as Nuestra Señora de Solentiname, that I soon learned was an international crossroads of artists, religious seekers, and revolutionaries. Several Nicaraguan painters were in residence, as well as a Mexican poet and a wandering archaeologist. During the month I

· · · · · ·

was there, I also observed the life of the peasants who lived in the islands as a community of believers attempting to liberate themselves from the twin tyrannies of State and Church. I felt no personal connection to what I saw. Like so many others who came through, I was a kind of tourist. On Saturday mornings, peasants from the islands came to Nuestra Señora de Solentiname to be instructed on the porch of the community's main house. While I was there, they were discussing a book about Marxism and Christ that I had never heard of. I was astonished, however, that peasants would willingly gather to talk about any book, much less one that sounded like a philosophical treatise.

On Sunday mornings before Mass, I joined in the soccer games played in a cow pasture beside the church whose roof was supported only by irregularly placed poles. Cows wandered in during Mass. Although I knew very little Spanish, I sat with the other players, smelling as they did of cow manure, and tried to follow the service. At the time of the sermon, Ernesto took off his vestments and lit a cigarette. He sat in front of the congregation, smoking, while he and they discussed the morning's Gospel lesson. (Later, I was able to understand the content of these dialogs, because some of them were published in three English volumes as *The Gospel in Solentiname*.) In the discussions, Ernesto encouraged the people to apply what they had heard in the Gospel to their daily lives. In particular, he often asked them to relate the Gospel to the injustice they were suffering under the dictator Anastasio Somoza. The Bible, in these discussions, was about revolution.

I did not understand what was really going on in Nicaragua, either theologically or politically. I knew that there was a rebel group known as the Sandinistas. I did not know that Ernesto and many of the people who came weekly to Mass were part of that rebel movement.

When I left Solentiname, Ernesto accompanied me to Managua. The evening before we departed, he celebrated the Eucharist with me and the few permanent residents of the community. The elements of the Mass were rum and bread. Although I did not understand at the time how I was being fed, in this meal, as at the Cathedral four months earlier, I was eating my life.

The people who sat at the table with me thought of themselves as part of a religious community, but they were artists and rebels of the Spirit, not monks. I wanted to call them brothers the next day as we left, but my Spanish was almost as bad as it was when I arrived, and I used the wrong word. Instead of *hermanos*, brothers, I said: *hermoso*, which means beautiful. When the revolution broke out five years later, they were among the first to be killed.

2
. . . . . .

IT IS THE FEAST OF ST. STEPHEN, 1983, bitterly cold. Snow has been on the ground for most of the month of December. The pipes in our house have frozen. The windows are iced shut. My wife's sisters and their families are visiting for the holidays. They look at me in amazement as I struggle into my coat and head for the door.

"Where are you going?"

"To church."

I have been back in the Church for only three years, and they are not used to this piety that I think of as spiritual discipline. The car's motor turns over, reluctantly. My breath hangs in the air and does not disappear. The chapel at the Church of St. Martin-in-the-Fields has not warmed up by the time I arrive. The celebrant says he decided not to turn on the heat.

"We'll be done in thirty minutes." He grins. "Besides, the cold is good for your soul." We leave our coats on. He drapes a stole over his. A third person arrives, the other priest in the parish. She looks stunned by the cold. We stand close to the altar table, as if it were a hearth and we immobile stones. On this St. Stephen's morning we are truly—in that sneering phrase often applied to Episcopalians—the chosen frozen.

The Mass begins, and we are still. The words remain among us like ice crystals. Then the celebrant prays, "We offer you these gifts. Sanctify them by your Holy Spirit to be for your people the Body and Blood of your Son, the holy food and drink of new and unending life in him. Sanctify us also. . . ." This invocation, this calling of the Spirit, is a moment of deepest mystery and, not surprisingly, extended controversy in the history of the Church. What does it mean to say that the bread and wine become Body and Blood?

Stephen also calls on this same Spirit. I think about his stoning. His claim to see Jesus at

. . . . . .

God's right hand leads directly to his death. The stones break his body, spill his blood. It happens like this, according to the law: one of Stephen's accusers drags him to a hill outside the city and throws him down on his back; a second witness of his blasphemy drops a large stone on Stephen's chest; people in the crowd, who have come out to watch, finish him off with a volley of stones.

When the celebrant raises and breaks the consecrated bread, we look up at it. There is a moment of profound silence. We are frozen in time, locked in that space, enlightened. The Holy Spirit arrives abruptly. It is as if someone has flung open the door and burst into the room bringing all the cold of heaven. We are blown away, as Stephen is blown away. We yield our spirits, pass the bread and then the wine to each other. This presence enfolds the room so that our breath no longer crystallizes. All is changed, and we are changed: it is as if we shed our clothes and stand naked in the cold that is now God's cold. We are the Body and Blood, a consecrated people. It is what happens every time the Eucharist is celebrated. This presence fills the room whether we notice or not.

In the parish hall, holding hot cups of coffee, we say nothing for a while. Then one of the priests, I do not remember which, asks, "Did you feel it?"

We nod. We felt it.

3

WHEN MY SON NICHOLAS was an infant and cried to be fed during the night, my wife and I took turns with him. He is adopted and was not breast-fed. That meant that I also had the privilege of feeding him. I loved being able to do that, to take him out of his crib in the dark and carry him upstairs to the rocking chair. He was born in January and came to us at the age of five days. It was a holy thing to nurture him like that, in the silent dark. I had just returned to the Church, and everything for me was suddenly holy: formula, a creaky rocker, the street noises.

My memory of sitting up with him in the rocker is vivid. No real time has passed. I still can see his face in the shadows, eyes closed, contented as the moon.

One night, when he was finished, I picked him up and held him against my chest, as I usually did, and started down the stairs. My socked feet slid out from under me and I landed abruptly on my tailbone on the top step. I bounced, fell backward, and slid down the stairs to the second floor. I stayed on my back all the way, holding Nicholas against my chest. At the bottom I lay on the floor, breathing heavily, scared, and hurt. My back felt like someone had peeled the skin off of it. Nicholas was still asleep.

Good dads take it for their kids. They don't drop the kid and grab for the railing. Somehow I knew that. It's genetic, I suppose. I knew that I was supposed to die before the kids—and even for them, if it came to that.

On another occasion, somewhat later in his life, my son was standing on the tray of his high chair, dancing to some unheard rhythm. I spotted him across the room while I was cooking dinner. He was waving a wooden spoon. I cried out as he started to topple over, seemingly unaware or unconcerned that he was falling. I dove across the kitchen—yes, dove, flew through the air—my arms outstretched. I landed on my chest, slid, and caught him in my arms. He chortled and bonked me with the spoon.

When my wife and I decided to separate, we had one of those kitchen-table conversations in which we told Nicholas and his sister Ruth what was going to happen and said, "Now, this isn't your fault."

Nicholas, thirteen, laughed. "It's just like in the movies. You guys sound like a movie." Ruth cried and said, "But you promised you wouldn't get divorced."

While they were growing up, my children lived in Philadelphia, and I went to see them—or they came to see me in New York—almost every weekend. It wasn't easy keeping up with them, being a father at long distance. I did what most fathers do—I spent too much money entertaining them. We went out to eat. We went to a ton of movies. We played pool. We went roller-skating. All of this activity wasn't entirely new to them. When they were babies, I used to take them to the zoo almost every Saturday so that their mother could grade papers and prepare for her classes. If we didn't go to the zoo, we went to the park along the Schuylkill River to feed the geese and watch the boat races.

I wanted them to think of me—when they got to be adults—not as someone who left them, but as the guy who was there when they were young, someone they liked to be with, someone they could talk to.

Jesus came to tell us about the kind of relationship that we can have with each other and with God. And he did it in part by talking about his relationship to God, whom he called "*Abba*"—or "daddy." I don't think that Jesus wanted us to picture God as a man or father or patriarch when he used that word, but rather he wanted to explain what closeness might be possible between us and God. It is like the closeness a son might feel with a father. Or a daughter with a mother. Like that.

Human beings are made to be in relationship. They are made to be with others and to love and nourish them. The people who saw Jesus in the flesh and knew him as a human capable of caring came to a new understanding of God—one in which God exists with and for us, not only beyond us as something more powerful. God is with us. And after Jesus was gone, those who had felt the presence of God through him came to understand that in some way Jesus remained among them, as Spirit.

In time, these different ways of being with God came to be understood as the Trinity—Father, Son, and Holy Spirit. The idea has become more complex than it needs to be.

The Trinity is about God as love, God in relationship.

There is a wonderful icon painted by Andrei Rublev in the early fifteenth century that shows three people seated at a round table. These people are neither male nor female. Each looks to the right and points to the next person, so that around the table they are forming a web of relatedness. This icon is about the Trinity. It is the clearest explanation I know for this abstract and otherwise not very interesting idea—that God is three persons in one.

But when I think of this icon, what I see behind these three people seated in the kitchen is me in midair diving toward my falling child. I see me come up holding the child who has not been hurt and who will one day hold me when I am dying.

4

· · · · · ·

I AM IN A BOAT WITH JESUS on the Sea of Galilee as a storm comes up. There are no other disciples with us. Jesus is sleeping in the prow. He looks serene. I am doing a good job of sailing, slicing against the wind. My hand holds the tiller fast, the sheet taut. The boat heels over, and I balance it by hiking over the water that rips by. I wish Jesus could see how good I am. It has been a long time since I last sailed—and never mind that no fisherman in Galilee had anything like this sloop.

But the clouds are coming fast across the lake with little warning, as apparently they do on the Sea of Galilee. The weather can be rough, the squalls fierce. I begin to get worried as the waves grow in size and the boat wallows in the deepening troughs. The sail dumps its wind. We are suddenly sideways against the rolling water, but I bring the boat about and catch enough wind to climb back into our tack. No problem. I can do this. But then a wave washes over and nearly capsizes us. I lose control of the sail altogether. We are at the storm's mercy, and in moments Jesus and I will both be in the water.

Absurdly, I wonder if Jesus can swim. I know I can. Will I have to rescue him?

He is still in the prow asleep. It is too much. I scream at him to wake up! And he does, right away. And when his eyes open, the storm disappears. The sea is flat. We are becalmed. The sun beats on us. He smiles and, for a moment, I want to leap across the boat and strangle him.

He is eating an apple now. He tilts his head back to feel the sun on his face.

"Can I ask you something?"

He looks at me. "Sure. Anything." He has a mouth filled with apple.

"Did you really rise from the dead?"

· · · · · ·

I expect him to be angry with me for asking such a stupid question. But he begins to laugh. It is the funniest thing he has ever heard. He chokes on the apple, spewing pieces of it onto his chest. But he says nothing. When the laughter passes, he just looks at me, his eyes still amused. He takes another bite of the apple.

And then I am lying beside him in the boat. We are like lovers now, our arms around each other. It is as if we have been sleeping and are just waking. I feel that nothing can touch me, that there is no danger. Jesus and I are together here at the center of the universe. Around us revolve all things. Nothing else matters but lying here in the sun.

This was not a dream. I entered this boat with Jesus while on retreat in the early '80s. My retreat director encouraged me to imagine myself to be part of certain Gospel stories, to talk to Jesus, to take part in them. Although I did not have much success—and on one occasion had a frightening encounter with a Jesus figure on the cross who looked like Quasimodo, as played by Charles Laughton—on this one day it seemed that I left my skin and my place in time behind.

My body remains in a grotto on the grounds of a Jesuit retreat center. My spirit is sailing with Jesus.

Jesus turns to me and says, "Whenever you need me, you can find me here."

5

TWO DREAMS confirmed for me that I am called to be a deacon in the Church. They came on successive nights one August during my year of vocational discernment in my Philadelphia parish. The members of the ministry committee all felt certain that I was not called to be a priest, but during the August vacation break we agreed to spend prayerful time on the question before concluding our work in September. It had been a good year together, a model for group discernment, and I felt lucky that these people had given so much of their time to my vocation in ministry.

Dreams have seldom been important to me, but on occasion they have been signs, I believe, of the presence of the Spirit. They have shown me a way, sometimes by frightening me. These dreams, however, were holy confirmations.

In the first, I am standing in a bakery shop, obviously in France. It has the distinctive look of a patisserie. I like French food, and France, and so this image is appealing. Quickly, however, I find myself in difficulty. I am trying to order a loaf of French bread—one of those long, thin baguettes that never quite fit in any bag—but am mispronouncing the French word, *pain*. I stand in front of the display case, pointing emphatically, repeating the English word: pain, pain. The clerk does not understand what I want.

Jesus in the sacrament is bread for the world, and a deacon's ministry is in the world among the poor and those who are in pain. This bread is also who I am.

The second is like the first in also representing one of the elements of the Eucharist, consecrated wine. In this dream, I am a chalice bearer in St. Martin-in-the-Fields, my parish in Philadelphia. The priest is also carrying a chalice, oddly enough. His is filled with wine. Mine is empty. I follow along as he communicates the kneeling congregants. Then, when he stumbles and his chalice tilts, spilling wine, I thrust my cup under his and catch the wine before it hits the floor. Without missing a beat, I offer the chalice to the next person.

The deacon is the minister of the chalice. The priest consecrates the elements and gives the cup to the deacon in the Eucharist. Again, the image seems completely clear.

Here, the dreams say, is what you are to do: serve the world in Christ's body and the Church in Christ's blood. Be in both places at once.

This eucharistic spirituality, which is central to diaconal ministry, is seen most clearly, I think, in the Gospel of John. The signs that Jesus performs there, unlike the miracles of the Synoptic Gospels, point to eucharistic presence—the marriage at Cana, the woman at the well, the raising of Lazarus, the meal by the Sea of Tiberias. Here is the Spirit of Christ in the world.

The dreams are not "messages" from God so much as confirmations of God's will mediated through others, in this case through the Church. The Spirit shows me to myself, as in a mirror suddenly cleansed of mist. That self I recognize was always there in some form, but only through prayerful discernment, through listening attentively to the voice of the Spirit, through paying attention can I see who I am. This is not work we do alone. Nor is it lacking in risk. In giving ourselves over to others in community, we act in faith that the Spirit is active in the world, that there is indeed one who knows us.

6

By the Sea of Tiberias, Peter says to several disciples who are with him, "I am going fishing." And they reply that they will go with him. So they get into the boat, but that night they catch nothing. Just after daybreak, they see a figure standing on the shore, but at first they do not know who he is. This man tells them to drop their nets on the other side of the boat—and they haul in a large quantity of fish. Peter realizes that it is the resurrected Jesus and leaps into the water to swim ashore.

This chapter in John's Gospel is tacked on at the end, an extra appearance narrative that ties up a few loose ends. It is about getting on with life, at least in part. How shall we live in this world after Jesus has been here and gone?

Well, Peter goes back to work. It is the most mundane of responses, but what else can we do after the excitement has died down, after the party's over? We go back into the world we came from, pick up the tools of our trades, provide for ourselves and others through labor. Jesus appears, as he usually does, while people are doing something else. Peter and the disciples are not at prayer. They are not gathered in one of the house churches singing hymns or sharing a meal. They are at work.

It is where we are most of the time, and yet we do not look for God there, as a rule, nor do we expect God to show up. The Holy Spirit is seldom welcome at a staff meeting or on a factory line. When we wish to encounter God, we like to select the appropriate place and even time. We go on retreat or for a walk in the woods, assuming that the Spirit will be where the Spirit belongs, in places of holiness, solitude, beauty.

Peter goes fishing because he is a fisherman. Jesus calls him while he is working and now, after his death and resurrection, Peter assumes there is nothing left for him but work. And in a sense he is right. Jesus calls the disciples in for a breakfast he has prepared—his fish, apparently, not one of theirs on the grill—and then following this Communion he introduces Peter, and indeed all of us, to the new work of the kingdom: love me, feed my sheep. Vocation is not something we choose. When you were young, Jesus tells Peter, you could make your own choices, go where you wished. That is what the young can do. But now I am calling you to assume the identity given you that is not a matter of choice.

Without vocation we are simply going through the motions—and, of course, many people spend their lives ignorant of their own vocational identity. They are not enlightened, to use the image from Buddhism. They have not encountered the truth of things. Peter goes back to work, it seems, still ignorant of the truth of things. That may be why this additional chapter has been added to John's Gospel. Jesus is raised from the dead. He is no longer with us. Now what?

Each of us is called to a common vocation, as John makes clear in 21:22. Peter is called to radical discipleship. It is the meaning of radical discipleship. Following Jesus is not something we do for a while and then return to work. It is not a break in the action. In following him, we find the one we are called to become. It is seldom what we want.

. . . . . .

7

THE MEN ARE NAKED ABOVE THE WAIST, except for the black hoods covering their heads. Their pained eyes stare through slits in the cloth. They carry on their shoulders bundles of staves, the thorns of which cut the flesh. Blood trickles down their backs as they struggle under the weight and strain of carrying their burdens up the hill. In front of them, women in black shuffle along on their knees, carrying lighted candles that drip hot wax on the cobblestones. Their knees and legs are scraped and burned.

It is Good Friday in Taxco, Mexico. Tourists crowd the town to watch the *penitentes* process through the steep streets, as they do every year. We watch in grim fascination. Most of us are Anglos to whom the parade makes little sense. We cannot imagine being inside a religion that leads people to abuse themselves like this.

Taxco is a picturesque village in the mountains south of Cuernavaca, where I have been studying Spanish in an intensive program for a week. Known primarily for its silver crafts, on this one day of the year the town becomes medieval. The silver shops are filled with shoppers. We take pictures. We shiver with dread. We shop and gape.

Holy Week for me has always been a time marked by intense emotions. By the end of the day on Good Friday, I feel as if someone close to me has died. I am despondent and spend Holy Saturday in a mourner's daze. It is a state I willingly enter in order to identify more fully with Jesus' pain, but I do not enter it out of a sense of my worthlessness before God or to demonstrate my abject sinfulness as it seems to me these men and women do. But the truth is, I do not understand them, who they are or why they are walking this way of the cross.

Seeing them does remind me that I live in a fallen world and that I, like them, am part of it. These suffering men and women are like all of those who suffer. They are broken by sin, which they carry like these bundled staves. They show us the interior of a world where terrors are fully exposed, where hatred is palpable, where weeping is no longer hidden. They show me something of the inside of my own fear. I cannot imagine doing what they do, but I understand what it feels like.

Jesus died for us to release us from fear, but here it is in front of me and, I realize, inside of me. Even though the resurrection sets us free, has set us free, we sometimes choose to walk in pain. Why dramatize it like this, I ask myself as the seemingly endless procession passes. It is reality as ritual. Tourists pull out their cameras. They point and shoot. I also take a photograph: a man's raked back. I do it to declare their strangeness. I do not want to be part of them.

As we say in the Eucharist, "Christ has died, Christ is risen." It has happened. The Spirit is with us. And yet the ritual re-enactment of the Passion reminds us of the precarious state of our lives so that we can understand the human Jesus who dies and is raised in affirmation of our humanity.

There are days when I drag myself out of bed convinced of my uselessness. I remember all that I have left undone, those I have wounded. The past sometimes overwhelms me. I suspect that all of us feel this way on occasion. Our selfishness and our greed are part of our inheritance. There are days, I understand, when I am just like these men and women. But God has looked at that, at the worst in us, and freed us of the burden through the death and resurrection of Jesus.

Watching these men and women as they make their wretched, holy way to the cathedral at the center of Taxco, I pray for all of us walking this world's bloody streets.

. . . . . .

8
. . . . .

THE KINGDOM of God is like this.

There are white mayflies swarming over the river in a frenzy of reproduction. The sun has slipped below the ridge. The surface of the river is alive with feeding fish. They are gorging on the mayflies that are laying eggs on the water. On the tippet (a thin, nylon filament at the end of the fly line), I tie an artificial fly that seems to be the same size, color, and shape of the flies electrifying the evening.

The fish we want to catch are across the river in a deep run by the far bank. They are forty feet away. My casting skills are good at thirty feet, but doubtful much beyond that. My friend is a master. He has taught me how to do this. We work together at Rutgers University. On Fridays we often slip away early to spend the afternoons until dark at the fishing club we belong to in western New Jersey. We like to fish until the bats come out. The river, rich with insect life, is full of large, fat, brown trout. They are educated fish that know artificial flies when they see them. But all of the members of the club are excellent anglers, who can bring inanimate flies to life. Together, fish and angler are like the hosts of heaven, doing their perfect dance in God's presence. I want to be part of that company.

My friend easily places his fly in the run, but the fish refuse to take. My casts fall short. But I am exhilarated by the vibrancy of the moment. Life and death surround us. The water pushes against our legs. My arm aches from casting. My heart is racing.

We have been fishing for four hours but have caught nothing. It is not unusual to fish four hours and catch nothing. Sometimes, the fish take every fly recklessly. On the best fishing day of my life, in Central Pennsylvania, I caught seventeen trout. I never keep them. We call it "releasing" the fish.

. . . . . .

None of this means a thing. We tell ourselves that catching fish is equal to not catching fish. But I still want to prove to my friend that I can drop a fly in that distant run and take a fish before he does. This is a guy thing. On an impulse, I decide to tie on a new artificial fly. My friend looks at me.

"What's that?"

I tell him. The fly has a name: "cream variant." I have never used this fly before. He shakes his head. It takes me several tries to tie it on. The light is low. My eyes do not focus. My hands twitch. Finally, I attach the fly, flick it back and forth over my shoulder, lengthening the line until I have forty feet in the air. It unrolls perfectly. The fly lands in the run, exactly where I wanted to put it, exactly where a fish had risen a moment before. I know what is going to happen. It is as if I *will* it to happen. I feel the hit in my shoulder, in my gut.

I have worked at doing this right. The fish is big, nineteen inches, hanging for a silver moment in the twilight as it leaps. I only want to see it in my hand, the beauty of its markings, deep colors along its flanks.

The wild eye fixes me. The mouth is working. I slip the hook from the corner of its mouth. The fish flexes and flashes back into the river.

The air is still alive with white flecks. It is almost like a snowfall. And then, suddenly, before I can cast again, the mayflies are gone. The fish stop feeding.

· · · · · ·

9

I WAS TEACHING A COURSE on publishing at the China Normal University in Shanghai when I learned of Scott's death. The incongruous setting of the student union made the news I heard through the public telephone all the more bizarre: "Scott O'Brien is dead." It would be incomprehensible under any circumstances.

Walking back toward my dormitory, I thought about our last year together. I wandered into the garden at the center of the campus and stopped on an arched bridge over a pond. It felt like a good place to reflect on life and death. Students brushed by, seeming not to notice me, but I knew they were acutely aware of my presence. Across the pond, I could see the young man assigned to keep an eye on me pause to watch. It was always hard to be alone in China.

Learning about Scott's death so far from home was painful. The funeral was to take place before I returned. Already I missed being with the people at our parish who had been so important in my spiritual life. Rector of St. Martin's in Philadelphia, Scott in his early forties was vibrant, funny, disorganized, and (as it happened) troubled. As my marriage was coming apart, so was his. As I began the process of discernment for ordination, he was leaving parish ministry to explore a long-suppressed vocation to write. We joked about trading roles. I was in love with the idea of ordination. It was hard for me to imagine how he could give up his ministry. But he was in love with the idea of being a writer, and I had all but ceased to write. He did not understand how I could do that.

The year before he died, Scott asked me to teach him fly fishing. We got together one Saturday in the backyard of the rectory with a couple of bottles of Yuengling ale. It was a cool spring day. I demonstrated the proper way to cast a fly line, more difficult than it seems.

22

While we cast, we talked about what was happening in our lives, the changes we anticipated. I knew that I would be leaving Philadelphia. He knew that he would be leaving the parish. But we had not yet told each other. Our talk was about our aspirations, his as a writer, mine as a deacon. I could tell that he did not really want to learn fly fishing.

The next Saturday I took him out to Valley Forge Creek, north of Philadelphia, which has a population of wild brown trout. We prowled the banks for a couple of hours. Scott caught a small fish, which made the trip worthwhile for me. I wanted him to catch fish.

He died of an embolism while driving through New York State to a writer's conference. He had not yet found a voice, and I mourned that loss as much as the loss of someone I loved.

My Shanghai keeper suddenly appeared at my elbow and asked if I felt all right.

"This pond is green," I said to him. Uniformly covered with algae so perfect it seemed artificial, the pond looked like a golf green, solid enough to walk on. I had wanted to ask about this strange phenomenon since my arrival. In my imagination, this was a kind of elegant Chinese pun: water transformed into earth.

Since I could not tell my keeper what I was feeling, I posed to him my theory about the algae-covered pond.

He looked puzzled when I asked him if my guess was correct.

"No," he said. "We try to get rid of the algae. It is very ugly."

10

IN THE EPISCOPAL CHURCH deacons, when present, read the Gospel at the Eucharist. It is the one distinct liturgical office that separates us from priests and laity.

This formal reading of the Gospel by one ordained to do it is also one of the marks of Catholic or sacramental worship. Just as the second part of the service is focused on the Communion, the first part—the Liturgy of the Word—revolves around the reading of the Gospel, the proclaiming of the Good News. Not even the sermon is more important. It is in the Protestant Free Church tradition that the sermon assumes primacy.

And so the reading of the Gospel is done with ceremony, often with candles and incense in procession. It is a solemn matter. When people ask me if I wish I were a priest so that I might celebrate the Eucharist, I reply that I am grateful to be a deacon so that I might read the Gospel.

Mark is close to the heart of deacons. His driving energy, concrete imagery, and insistent language remind us of the lives we lead—both in the Church and in the world, dashing back and forth between the two. In Mark, Jesus does things suddenly. He is immersed in the everyday life of his society. He heals, he feeds, he takes care of people. And deacons are called to emulate this active Jesus.

The Gospel opens with "the good news of Jesus the Anointed" and suddenly we are by the River Jordan where "John the baptizer" has been conjured by a quotation from Isaiah the Prophet. And then Jesus is there. He is baptized. The Spirit descends. And right away the Spirit "drives him out into the wilderness." A verse later, John is locked up, and Jesus is preaching in Galilee.

My life feels just like that, as if there is no time between events, as if I were driven by the Spirit. There seems to be no time for transitions. But life without pauses becomes tangled. Even deacons need to stop moving. The Benedictine tradition teaches monks to stop between actions—the word is *statio*, that still place where we have finished what we were doing but have not yet begun to do something new. We mark the boundary in order to honor our place in the flow of work—and indeed to honor the work itself. In Mark, Jesus also seeks *statio*. He rises early while it is still dark and goes out of the house to an isolated place to pray. And so, although he is in constant motion, we see him early in the story alone and in prayer and know that this is the pattern of his life.

At the midpoint of the Liturgy of the Word—after the opening collect, the creed, the reading of the lessons and the psalm—I take the Gospel book from the altar, where I have placed it at the beginning of the service, and carry it in front of my face into the congregation. All is still. This is the moment of *statio* in our lives when we stop doing everything so that the word of God can come into us. Everyone stands. All eyes are fixed on the gospeler. But it is not the deacon they see; rather, it is the Christ who manifests the Good News. He is the Gospel. Just as the identity of the priest who celebrates the Eucharist is unimportant, so too the one who reads the Gospel disappears into the body of Christ. It is the moment in time when the divine breaks into human history. All that has happened is forgotten, In a sense, there is no future. There is only this holy now.

· · · · ·

11

· · · · · ·

For a while I was responsible one Sunday a month for Morning Prayer at St. Luke's Hospital in Manhattan, where I was a volunteer chaplain. The services were broadcast live on closed-circuit television and then rebroadcast in patients' rooms throughout the next week. The main chapel is a beauty. Emphatically Episcopal, it was built when hospital workers and patients went to church on Sundays and even during the week. Now, the balcony, which once held the choir, is used for services because it is smaller, the space more intimate. The stained-glass wall above the altar of the big chapel forms a glittering background for the camera.

Because I believed my singing did not inspire holiness, I usually took along with me one or two people from my home parish as a "choir." One Sunday, I invited a resident of the AIDS care center our parish sponsors to join me. George had had a stroke in the past year and was in a wheelchair, although he was able to walk short distances with the aid of a cane. He had briefly sung professionally, but his effort to make it as an entertainer ended when he was diagnosed with HIV. For a period following the stroke, he had to wear diapers.

When I arrived to pick him up, he was eating breakfast, wearing a white band-collar shirt with rhinestone buttons. At his neck was his mother's butterfly broach, which he always wears, he told me, when he performs. Completing the outfit was a cream satin jacket trimmed in gold. I noticed what appeared to be bloodstains on one of the sleeves. In the town car that came to pick us up, George rode as if he were rich and famous, a regal tilt to his head. He complained—for the moment a petulant dandy—about the nurses who were

· · · · · ·

not available to help him dress that morning. Then, ashamed of his pose, he admitted his bad mood and promised to get over it.

"We have the Lord's work to do," he said.

The expected volunteers were not in the chapel to pick up patients, although the cameraman was there setting up his equipment. When a nurse called to tell us she had a patient who wanted to come to church, I went to get him, leaving George to greet worshipers and practice the hymns he selected. The organist, who was also a security guard at the hospital and usually reliable, had not yet arrived. As I went down the hall, already vested, I could hear George warming up. He had a sweet voice that calmed my nerves.

Wearing my alb in the hospital made me feel like someone from another planet. A doctor on the elevator took a long look at my hospital identification. I wanted to say, "I am an angel," but restrained myself. I gave him a holy gaze.

The patient was named Timothy. He was thin and shaky. He walked slowly. In addition to cancer, he had AIDS and was trying to stay off heroin. By the time we got back to the chapel, we had only a couple of minutes before the service was scheduled to begin. There was one other person in the congregation, a nurse who also was with me the morning a patient threw up as I began to preach.

In my homily, I quoted Henri Nouwen, who wrote that the vocation of the minister is to make connections between the human story and the divine story. The story we bear as Christians is the one that shows us how healing begins in the recognition that our human wounds are those of the suffering God. The issue for us as servants of others is not taking their pain away but showing it to them as part of what Nouwen calls the greater pain, which includes our own.

After the service, the nurse hugged and thanked me. We all hugged each other, except

. . . . . .

for the cameraman who darted off to do an errand before the Catholics came in. I left the candles lit for them.

George was giving Tim advice. "Trust in God. Take your troubles to the Cross. It will work out."

An early arrival for the Catholic service overheard and said to me, "If only it was really like that."

"It is like that," I told her. "That's why we're here."

George and I walked Tim back to his room, where he held me against his chest and wouldn't let go.

12

GOD CALLS ME to be with the dying. I do not know why. It has not always been so. In the beginning of my training for the diaconate, I did not do well with the short course we had to take in hospital-based chaplaincy (known as "clinical pastoral education"). At the time, nothing about caring for the sick appealed to me. I did my eight weeks and moved on, grateful to be through with hospitals, I hoped, forever. Between that first exposure to caring for the sick and the realization that God wanted me to be with the sick, I lost both job and marriage, and it felt as if much of what had anchored me had been blown away. I hit bottom. When I began a second pastoral training program in New York, I understood instantly what was being asked of me. A friend in my class during that first dreadful experience laughed when I told her I was a volunteer chaplain at St. Luke's Hospital.

"Don't you just love God's sense of humor?"

No one close to me has died in my life, although I have grieved for lost relationships, for people I no longer see who once were important to me. When my father's mother died—she was not someone I knew as a grandmother—I tried to talk to him about it. I wanted to know what it was like for him to lose her. This conversation took place soon after my parents had spent a long weekend with me and my therapist trying to open some closed doors between us. It was my first attempt to talk to my father (on my own) about something important.

I knew that he and his mother had not been close. When he spoke of her, he invariably recalled how she always favored his brothers, even when he was the one supporting the family during the Depression. I could tell he thought she had not been grateful enough. Growing up, I knew she was a hard-edged woman. We all knew that, but I did not know her except through him. Throughout my life, she lived across the country in Arizona, and when she died I had not seen her in fifteen years.

I asked my father how he was doing. We were talking on the telephone.

"I'm OK," he snapped, suggesting there was no other way to be. It was a voice he had practiced.

"I mean it must be hard," applying therapy's hard-won lessons. Be direct. Say what you mean.

"It's not hard. She's dead."

I realized that I wanted him to mourn out loud, to admit that he cared. I suppose he was also being direct. He said what he meant, not what I wanted.

"But now both of your parents are gone." His father died many years earlier. I did not remember him at all.

"So?"

There was a long pause. In my mind, I asked if he wanted me to say that about him when he was gone, but I understood that I was afraid of the answer. The real question was what he would say if I were gone. At the time, I did not know that. I only felt this inexplicable grief for this woman I scarcely knew, who was part of my life but a stranger.

"Look," he said, "she never really liked me. She always preferred Don. We haven't gotten along for years. It's like . . . to me . . . she died a long time ago. So this is not really important. You don't have to worry about it."

But I do worry about those who die alone, and I want to be there with them and those they leave behind. In the presence of the dying we are free to be ourselves. There are no conditions, nothing to forgive. All that matters is this moment we share as life elides into death, when there are no consequences and everything has already happened.

Everyone I visit is my father's mother.

13
· · · · · ·

As an editor and writer, I live surrounded by books. I buy them. I buy a lot of them. I think I began to be like this in college, when my Greek and English History professor met his classes in his home, a small, book-filled cottage on the campus, located behind the library. I wanted to have his life, which included an antique English sports car and devotion to the Queen and Church of England (at Lynchburg College, a school run by the Disciples of Christ, a denomination I recall as Low Church Methodism). One day he said to me, as I worried about whether I could afford to buy a book I wanted, "In life, you should never think about the cost of books or good wine. They are," he said, "like air." That is all the justification I needed. For years, my money has gone first for books, then for wine, sometimes in reverse order. All else comes last.

There was a time in my life when I had a cellar of good wines for others to admire. I drink less wine these days and live in a high-rise apartment without a cellar. My library is scattered in several locations now, the bulk of it in the house my former wife occupies in Philadelphia. My apartment in New York is too small for my entire library. Some of my favorite books are there, some in the basement storage bin. Another part of the collection is in a hallway closet on the penthouse floor of the apartment building. My parish office houses my religion library. Most of the books I acquired and edited as a publisher were left behind when I resigned as director of Rutgers University Press. My successor threw them away.

I used to think I could not live without being able to touch any one of my books whenever I wanted. Occasionally, I catch myself looking for a book I know I own but that is lost in some remaindered part of my life. I reach for it and then remember that it is somewhere else. How can I own it if I cannot touch it? Who is the owner? Who is owned? I imagine

· · · · · ·

these books as pieces of myself lying along the road. They are curiosities, somehow part of me but no longer who I am. Leaving them around in the landscape is a way of saying that I was there.

I have bought books out of a restless need to own and to do in order to be. Books have completed me in ways that I do not fully understand. Most of the books I bought I did not need. Some I have not even read. They are there, I tell myself, in case I need them. But where am I in these stacks? I fear that too often the books have kept me from confronting myself: the work that is not only in my head, what I am in the world. They have invited me to retreat from the world, to create myself in my own image. Like other work, the books have allowed me to be almost anyone but the one others need me to be.

I have come to believe that the work of the last half of my life is to discover who I am for others. It is different from the work that once defined me, which depended so completely on the printed word as a measure of who I was for myself.

When I lost the job that was the capstone of my career as a publisher, I thought I had lost my identity. For twenty-eight years I had done this one thing. That was how people recognized me. This new anonymity showed me myself.

St. Francis once insisted that the friars give up every book, even the Bible. "This is all you need," he said, dumping ashes on his head. He was not illiterate and yet he rejected books as primary ways of knowing. He wanted to kick the props out. He insisted that people be wholly *with* each other. Jesus did that too. In the first years after I returned to the Church, I became a novice in the Third Order Franciscans, drawn as much as anything by Francis's joy in the created world. But this other part—giving up everything, especially books—bothered me, and I did not become a member of the Order. I was like the rich young ruler who could not give up his many possessions.

But I long to sit in the ashes with others.

· · · · · ·

14
. . . . . .

ROBERTA KNOWS she is dying. She has AIDS. Her mother sits on one side of the hospital bed; I am on the other. I hold Roberta's hand. Her mother looks away.

"I guess this will show you. I told you how many times? But you never listen. Now maybe you will." Her mother glares at me. "She was always a rebellious child."

Her mother's grief comes out in anger. Roberta's eyes are pleading with me: Get rid of her. But she says, "What's it like to die?"

I don't know. Before I can attempt an answer, Roberta begins screaming, thrashing on the bed. I hold her down. The nurse rushes in, injects her with a sedative. To my surprise, the nurse then sits on the side of the bed and strokes Roberta's hair. I take her hand again.

The nurse says, "It's going to be all right, honey. Don't think about anything. God takes care of you."

Dying is like that, I realize. The nurse knows what I am supposed to know but could not say. I forget sometimes that the simple answers are usually the right ones.

Two days later, I visit Roberta while she is on a dialysis machine. She smiles in weak recognition. Her mother is nowhere to be seen, and I am guiltily grateful. I ask if she is hungry.

"No. But I want some water."

I get her a cup of water with a flex straw. She sips, then says she wants some pudding. I give her three or four spoonfuls before she turns her head away.

"I've been praying for you," I tell her.

She looks at me in surprise. "Me?"

She dies two hours after I leave.

● ● ●

. . . . . .

Another AIDS patient I have come to know, improbably named Mercy, goes the same way. She has been in our hospital before, but I somehow understand that this time she is here to die. She shows no interest in the long talks we had during her first stay here. Now she just lies in bed. "Bless me," she says, and, after I do, does not speak during my subsequent visits. When I make the sign of the cross on her forehead, she closes her eyes in surrender.

During the next week, she is often sleeping when I visit. I sit by her bed, touch her forehead. Often, she catches me watching her, eyes opening abruptly, as if she were not sleeping at all. Sometimes I feel reproach in her stare.

She dies on an evening when I am somewhere else.

• • •

Tom is unable to speak. He probably has AIDS, but I do not know. Emaciated, weak, he simply watches me as I read to him from the psalms. Every now and then, he lifts a hand and points. He wants me to look at something, but all I see is the blank wall. The nurses tell me that he is to be moved in a few days to a long-term-care facility. He will live a long time like that, they say. It seems a horrifying prospect.

The last time I see Tom, he is sleeping. I say a prayer over him and start to leave. He wakes suddenly. I say, on impulse, "Do you want me to give you Communion." He nods. I give him a small piece of host. It sits on his tongue, which protrudes from his mouth for a minute. I wonder briefly if he knows what I have given him. Then he swallows. He raises his hand and points across the room.

"I see it, Tom. I see it." I make the sign of the cross on his forehead and leave. He dies that night.

· · · · · ·

15

WORK IS A RECURRING IMAGE in the Gospels, not only in the lives of the people but in the stories Jesus tells. When we first meet Jesus' disciples in the Synoptic Gospels, a few of them are identified by the work they do. Simon and Andrew, fishermen, are casting a net into the lake; James and his brother John are in the fishing boat with their father Zebedee, mending their nets. Matthew is in his tax-collector's booth. We know Joseph as a carpenter (Matthew 13:55) and in popular imagination see Jesus as a young boy working with his father. Work cuts across boundaries because everyone does it. And human work is a vehicle for understanding how God works.

When he comes along, Jesus radically changes the nature of the work of those who follow him. The disciples fish for people. Jesus also has new work to do. He is no longer a carpenter. He heals. He preaches. Jesus tells the disciples in Mark that they are going to the "neighboring towns, so that I may proclaim the message there also; for that is what I came out to do" (Mark 1:38). One of the major conflicts Jesus has with the temple authorities is over the work one is allowed to perform on the Sabbath, the sign of the Creator's rest from the work of creation. Where their view is restrictive, his is expansive.

I have tried at various times in my life to "keep the Sabbath" by refraining from work on Sunday. It is difficult to do. Fifty- to sixty-hour workweeks are common for me. I usually devote another twelve hours to the Church in my role as a deacon and volunteer chaplain. Sunday can be the most exhausting day of the week—five hours at the church, another hour or two visiting the sick. In our work-dominated culture, I suspect that too many of us have similarly hectic working lives, consuming half of each twenty-four-hour day, intruding randomly on our so-called free time. Telephones and computers keep us constantly connected to our jobs.

Jesus offers a different perspective on work. It should not be something artificially split from life. It is integral to who we are. Our work is somehow in us waiting to be called into being, but it cannot limit what we do, as it does in so much of our culture. In this view, keeping the Sabbath is not about identifying the one day of the week on which we do no work, or the one day of the week on which we worship. Rather, it is cultivating an attitude that allows us to do what we need to do, human work and worship, wherever we are and on whichever day of the week. To pass an hour in a church on Sunday and the rest of the day in idleness, perhaps watching television or ingesting a giant meal, is not in itself an observance of Sabbath.

Work and worship are equally important to holy living. We have separated the two, relegating worship to a small piece of each week and giving ourselves wholly to the notion of work as secular activity, thereby demeaning worship as well as work. In an odd way, the struggle to keep the Sabbath as a day set apart has reinforced this idea. Our Sundays have become prisoners of the secular.

Jesus works on the Sabbath. He prays during the week. He calls his disciples not to abandon work but to put on a new work, one that allows them to be more completely themselves—all the time, not only on Sunday.

All time belongs to God. All time is Sabbath.

· · · · · ·

16

· · · · · ·

As a deacon in an African-American parish, I try to spend part of one morning a week at the church in order to get to know the people in the community. Today, before meeting with the priest-in-charge there, I have breakfast with a young priest from another parish. We get together every now and then to complain about life in the Church. Sometimes he invites me to preach in his parish, which is also African-American. I use him as a sounding board, a reality check. He does not put up with brainless idealism, particularly of the white, liberal variety. That is another way of saying that he can be cynical. He helps me understand the race politics of Harlem and the Church.

Today I tell him about my resentment toward the priests in my parish. It has been building for a couple of days, as it sometimes does when I think that they do not appreciate what I do. (At the altar last week, one pronounced the dismissal, a part of the liturgy reserved for deacons, and explained later, "I forgot you were there," smiling ruthlessly. What I call "the struggle over the liturgy" takes up a lot of psychic energy in the Church.) All deacons are assailed by feelings of resentment every now and then. It is our characteristic anxiety. Because we cannot preside at the Eucharist, priests and others in the parish often forget that we are equal members of the clergy (although most deacons are not paid to exercise their ministry.) The Church is hierarchical in practice, although not in theology, and it seems to be our human nature to want to climb to the top of heaps. Deacons—by their ordination— vow to remain where they are in the heap. (I had to sign a declaration saying I would never seek ordination to the priesthood.) They are ordained to deny hierarchy and to be powerless. It is easier said than done, for all clergy are assumed by the world to have power. Priests

· · · · · ·

are often suspicious of deacons' motives, assuming that no one would willingly surrender power. Some even believe that deacons are spies planted by bishops to inform on them.

My resentments this morning have specific causes, but I understand that they are not the problem. The problem is how we measure worth—how I measure my worth. I have to learn to resist my urgent need to be recognized and appreciated, to be powerful. Ordination does not confer this gift of humility; ordination requires that we seek it. It is another one of those divine paradoxes—that we are presumptuous enough to pray for humility.

After an unsatisfactory meeting with the priest-in-charge, and after failing to track down a parishioner I am supposed to meet who has not appeared, I am more resentful. The priest is a charismatic leader, and like many such people he can be autocratic. The deacon's job is to encourage lay ministry, but that is almost impossible to do in a parish in which the priests make unilateral decisions. And that is the case in too many parishes. The job of the deacon is to erode authoritarian structures. We are designated subversives.

On the train to my office in New Rochelle at noon, I reflect on a mostly wasted morning and try to come to terms with my resentment. Despite my best efforts, I continue to struggle with the condition of being a volunteer, of not being paid—or paid adequately or on time—for my work. It has been harder than I thought it would be. I depend on others for affirmation. God has made me a deacon perhaps because of that very fact: be a servant so that no one will affirm me.

· · · · · ·

17
. . . . . .

HE CATCHES MY EYE as I turn to leave the hospital room. He lies in the bed by the window, both of his legs stiff and bandaged. His roommate, the man I have been visiting, says, "You should talk to Red. He's lonely." It is the end of the day. I am tired and want to go home, but Red has a pleasant face, an engaging smile. I introduce myself.

"You're my angel," he says.

I don't feel like anyone's angel. My mind is troubled by debt, my children, work. But I try to focus on Red. "What happened to you?"

"I got hit by a car at Amsterdam and 125th. It came out of nowhere, hit me, and kept on going. At least, I guess that's what happened. I was out cold. But people saw it."

"Do you live up there?"

"Well, I live in the park...the Sheltering Arms. You know it?"

"Next to St. Mary's Church. That's my parish."

"No kidding! I go there on Mondays for the soup kitchen. That's my family. Imagine that! Are you a priest?"

We settle in to talk about the people we know at St. Mary's, life on the street in Harlem, Red's past. At some point, after losing a job, he dropped out. He admits to drinking a little, and I suspect that is the major reason he has ended up on the street. He has the emaciated look of someone whose major food group is alcohol.

"Do you have family in New York?"

"Nah. I've never had nobody really. Just me. I like it that way. I like living on the street, you know. The park is nice. Maybe not so much in the winter, but you get along. People are

. . . . . .

mostly pretty good to you if you leave 'em alone and if you're good to them. Except this guy that put me in here."

"No idea who hit you?"

"Well, my buddy Frank at the deli there on the corner, he saw it."

"Maybe he got a license number."

"Could be. The police came, but they don't do nothin', you know."

"I'll see what I can find out. A guy in the parish is a lawyer who might be able to help."

Red is ecstatic. The next day I call Jim, who refers me to a friend of his who is willing to look into getting Red some compensation. For a week, I visit Red every day. His gratitude buoys my own sagging spirits. Others from the soup kitchen go to see him when they find out he is in the hospital. But then he is transferred to a nursing home in the Bronx for rehabilitation. I do not see him again, although a couple of people from the kitchen go out there once or twice.

The lawyer looking into the accident calls me every so often. He is making progress, he says. He knows who hit Red. There might be an insurance settlement. Then, for several months, there is no news. I forget about it. My personal troubles are eased somewhat. I change parishes. Then, one morning about two years after I met Red, the lawyer calls to ask me if I know where he is. I do not.

"Call St. Mary's. Someone there will know. What's up?"

"Well, I've got some news for Red. Good news. We've got a settlement."

"Really. That's terrific. How much?"

"Probably about $90,000."

18
. . . . . .

TODAY IS ONE OF THOSE DAYS. I do the Sunday Morning Prayer service at St. Luke's Hospital, visit a frightened patient scheduled for by-pass surgery tomorrow, catch the train to New Rochelle to meet with Father Tissa Balasuriya (a priest from Sri Lanka whose book on Mary as a symbol of liberation got him in trouble with the Pope), return to New York for a meeting of the board of *Cross Currents* (the journal of interreligious affairs that I edit), and then attend a farewell dinner for that journal's retired, founding editor, Joseph Cunneen. It is not a day of rest.

And follows several days of restlessness. I have been driving my son around to visit art schools in Baltimore, Providence, and New York. We have a good time, the two of us, even though we drive nearly 1,000 miles in two days. We eat French fries and cheese doodles. He takes photographs from the car, experimenting with light.

He slouches across the back seat shooting up at an overhead toll-booth sign.

"The light's too dim," I call over my shoulder, paying the toll. I hit the gas as he snaps.

"DAD! I was taking a PICture." He flops over the front seat, looking forward.

"Nice sunset," I say.

"Yeah, well, who can take pictures, the jerky way you drive?"

Naturally, he especially likes the Rhode Island School of Design, the most expensive school on the tour. I know why he likes it. His instincts are usually pricey. But at the same time I think he will do better at a place like Pratt, which is as gritty as his politics. He is Chinese and adopted and identifies most closely with black kids and hip hop. His hair, in fact, is spiked for this trip—a new hairdo and, I can't help but think, a calculated statement of artistic nature. I can see that it is out of place at the professionally-oriented RISD. He looks just like the kids at Pratt, which we visit in New York at the end of our tour, but he likes it least.

When I leave to catch the train to New Rochelle, he heads off to take pictures in a street fair. Sometime this afternoon he will take the train back to Philadelphia, where he lives with his mother. My unusually busy day upsets me for this reason, too—we have to cut his visit short. As he grows older, I see less of him. When his mother and I separated, he was thirteen and I visited him and his sister (who is the same age) nearly every week. I work hard to maintain a relationship with them, despite my being in New York City. I fall into all of the distant-dad behaviors, spending too much money to entertain them.

Now that Nick is nearly nineteen, we talk more. We are less afraid of being angry. A sign of our deeper relationship: he calls when he gets back to Philadelphia, leaving a message on my machine that conveys affection. There is nothing much in it. "I'm home. Thanks for driving me around. Call me when you get the pictures."

On the trip back to New York from Rhode Island, we stop at the beach house on Block Island Sound that his mother and her two sisters own. It sits a hundred yards off a private beach flanked by rocks that hold striped bass. Most mornings when we went to the beach as a family for summer vacations, I counted on catching bass in the rocks. I went out before dawn with a fly rod and cast colorful "deceivers" (fishing lures that look like baitfish) into the choppy water the fish love. When one shagged the lure, he took form from the roiling water, the clash of surfaces, the movement, as if made of brine.

There is bright, low sun on the beach, and our shadows are long. The clean sand is rippled by wind. Nick takes pictures of the sand, a chimney left standing after the 1938 hurricane, and the corpse of a large sea turtle—bones stuck out from under the massive shell. He has never seen a sea turtle in the nearly nineteen years he has been coming to the beach. We think about how this one got here. I am always struck by the carnage on the beach. The sea turtle is just another body. The skeletal head of a bluefish lies nearby.

· · · · · ·

19

THE PETER PAN BUS takes me from the Port Authority Bus Terminal in Manhattan to what I call the Gas 'n' Go in Culpeper, Virginia, where my parents meet me. We drive from there to Madison, where they live. This part of Virginia is in the foothills of the Blue Ridge Mountains, which we can admire through the picture window on the west wall of the living room. It is a view my mother always wanted and now, in retirement, has. She and my father are where they want to be, in the dream house they built, and have no plans to leave, even though my father has Parkinson's and falls down occasionally. The volunteer rescue squad makes regular visits.

This Christmas I am spending two weeks with them. The journey south is a pilgrimage. The shrine at the heart of this pilgrimage is the family. At this time of the year, the American ideal is to make this pilgrimage, to go south or north with the kids so that the family can be together at Christmas. This image of the family Christmas is Victorian. We continue to hold it as an emblem of how we would like to live, several generations gathered together around a fire on a cold, snowy night. In Anglo-American culture, the Charles Dickens story "A Christmas Carol" is as central to our observance of the Incarnation as are the stories in Matthew and Luke. They are all good myths.

But there is more than the saccharine in the Gospel stories. Look at Matthew, where the three wise men travel a great distance to deliver gifts on the strength of a rumor. They are threatened by King Herod. There is real danger, as we learn when Herod begins slaughtering the young males. Joseph and Mary escape with Jesus to Egypt, leaving us that enduring image of pilgrimage: Mary on the donkey holding the infant as Joseph walks beside them. They are refugees from terror. Imagine them fleeing Kosovo or Rwanda. Remember, as we read the story, that it is a mirror of the Exodus, recalling slavery, years in desert exile, a protracted journey to a place of promise, a long deliverance from a place of bondage.

Pilgrimage is hard spiritual work, even when we are only going home. We begin in high spirits and arrive in foul humor. The Port Authority Bus Terminal is thick with desperate travelers. The bus smells of whatever disinfectant is used in its bathroom. A child has been screaming for several miles. A couple is arguing furiously. On overhead television screens *It's a Wonderful Life* imposes itself again on all of us. The bus grumbles into the Gas 'n' Go's empty parking lot near midnight at the intersection of strip-zoned highways.

Being home is never quite as wonderful as we think it will be. My father has a black eye from his most recent fall. Mom has back problems. And so we worry about how they will continue to take care of themselves up here on the hill outside of Madison. My own routine is broken; my normally peripatetic life stops here, although I bring work with me. Everyone can find me on e-mail. I settle into the rhythm of my parents' days, the ritual of breakfast and newspaper, the televised sports, the trips to the dump.

Once a week, dad meets a group of other men for breakfast at the McDonald's. I go along for a sausage biscuit with egg and talk about the fishing, if there is any. After the mudslides of two years ago, the Rapidan River (in the mountains no bigger than a creek) still has not come back; the brook trout are scarce. Time slows. I notice it first when the bus comes off of Route 66 to 29 at Gainesville. The speedy north slips away. I am in the South now, where the roomy land is tilled. There are more people in my apartment house in New York than there are in all of Madison.

Jesus came into the world to die. That is one way of clarifying the meaning of Incarnation. We all come into the world to die. The pilgrimage we make to family shrines is a way of circumventing our certain death. In the crucible of affection, we see continuity. The children carry on for us, just as we have carried on for our parents. We can believe that we are part of a journey that has meaning. The difficulty is in the sense that we *have* to make the trip. There is an obligation to be pilgrims, to suffer, to be annoyed, to overeat, to be with Aunt Emma. These are not trivial matters: they are the substance of life.

The relatives arrive. We sit around the fireplace while the Redskins play the Cowboys. We all hate the Cowboys. One of my sisters brings the ritual tin of popcorn, three flavors, enough for several days of munching. The children are there with the latest electronic games. There is family news, good and bad. There are stories retold. We eat and drink too much, gain weight. Too many presents circle the tree, which mom decorates each year with an accumulation of ornaments embodying over fifty years of this family's life. The tree joins the mountains in the picture window. It is the focus of the shrine.

When I was just out of college I avoided this annual pilgrimage. It was painful for my mother, I know. She wanted the children to be with her at Christmas, and I seldom was. In later years, I have come to think of the trip to Madison at Christmas as one that confers grace, as all pilgrimages should. Grace feels just like this: I get off the bus, stiff and disoriented. I am not sure whether I have arrived in Egypt or escaped from Egypt. There are dangers all around, as real as the rage of Herod. The night is dark. Snow begins to fall. I am standing in the parking lot of the Gas 'n' Go, asking myself, "What are you doing here?"

· · · · ·

20

· · · · · ·

AFTER BEING ORDAINED, I discovered that I can sing. I consider this a miracle and so do the members of my family. Deacons have traditionally been thought of as singers—and in fact one of the liturgical acts assigned particularly to deacons is the chanting of the Exsultet at the lighting of the Pascal Candle during the Easter Vigil. I had simply assumed that this was one diaconal function that I would have to forego. But I now expect to sing the Exsultet and do it reasonably well.

Even though I am terrified of singing loudly enough to be heard, even in a congregation singing hymns, I decided that on the Sunday following my ordination I would chant the Gospel, a challenge to my image of myself and a declaration of my identity as a deacon. I thought it might be the first and last time I soloed in church. I practiced with the choir director. She said I would be all right, but I could tell she had doubts. When the time came, I opened my mouth and throat and sang. Later, my mother and sister both said that their first thought was that someone was singing in my place. It was not great, they said, but it was perfectly acceptable.

Several months later I moved to a new parish, where the rector had a particularly good singing voice. I found myself seated beside her during services and, following her lead, began to enjoy singing. She said to me one day, knowing my concerns about my voice, "You know, sometimes you sing very well. When you're bad, you're terrible. But often you're right on key." I was astonished, but the comment lead me to be more confident in my singing.

For the Saturday evening Vigil service during the first Easter in my new parish, someone else sang the Exsultet, sparing me what I thought would be certain ignominy. But the next morning, Easter Sunday, I suddenly realized that, at the end of the service, I would be

· · · · · ·

expected to chant the complicated "Alleluia" that deacons sing each week during the Easter season. I had heard it sung, and in my head knew the sequence of notes, but I had not ever sung it myself—and certainly had not practiced. I asked the rector if she thought I should try it. She shrugged. It was, as far as she was concerned, up to me. When the Eucharist ended and the final hymn was finished, I simply did it.

After that, I sang the Easter dismissal with increasing confidence. Each time it was better. I could feel it. My hymns became increasingly tuneful. I began to enjoy singing—and that was completely new. Not long after Pentecost, the rector said in passing, "You know you actually have a lovely voice. You can sing, you know."

This was like discovering that I could fly. Within a year I had gone from being someone convinced of his inability to sing to one who is assured he has a lovely voice. The evidence around me is also convincing. I get no funny looks when I sing. I feel part of the music. Although I know that I depend on our rector, who sings beside me during the service, I also know that my increased confidence in myself has strengthened whatever natural ability I have.

A piece of diaconal identity that I assumed would not be mine I have discovered deep within. This is exactly what it means to have a vocation, I think. Inside of us is that piece of identity, that clarity of self, where who we are is what we do. What is easy is matching the obvious pieces. For me, some aspects of being a deacon have come naturally. Other pieces were missing, however, and I had simply decided nothing could be done about that.

I was wrong. I am still finding my voice.

21

. . . . . .

I SEE A MAN STANDING OUTSIDE of a room in the intensive care unit of the hospital. Because he looks distressed, I stop to talk with him. His mother has congestive heart disease. He fears she is going to die soon. He wants me to talk to her, help her come to terms with her death. He is in his thirties, his mother in her late sixties, too young to die. I go in to see her. Her skin is darker than I expected—and later I learn that she is part Hawaiian. I lean over and introduce myself. She rolls her head away from me.

At such times I feel tentative. I am invading her world now and have to be prepared to be rebuffed. This death is hers. She has exclusive right to it. I ask her if she would like me to pray with her. She nods her head, still turned away. I take her hand in mine. She looks at me, and there are tears on her cheeks. "Why are you crying," I ask.

"Because I was raped," she whispers.

At first, I think I have misheard, but she repeats what she said.

"When?" It feels like a stupid question, but my first thought is that she is talking about something that happened a long time ago.

"Yesterday."

"Here? In the hospital?"

She nods. I can think of nothing useful to say except in prayer, and so I pray for her in her pain and humiliation. Outside, I ask her son if what she has told me is true. It is. Another patient came into her room during the night and raped her. He was caught in the act by a nurse. Tomorrow the district attorney is coming to take a videotaped deposition so that they have what they need to prosecute before she dies.

. . . . . .

Her son is in agony. What if she is not strong enough to cope with an interrogation? Might giving the deposition—reliving the trauma—literally be fatal? Wasn't once enough? His mother was never one to talk about such things—and now on camera?

And so the two of us talk about what is to be done, to prepare her for the deposition and for death. For some reason, he has concluded that I can be helpful in both. He lets me into their lives. It is a great privilege and a fearsome responsibility. I feel small, and yet at the same time words come out that make sense to both of us. He asks me to come back the next day for the deposition.

When I return, the D.A. is in the hall outside the woman's room with an assistant, two police officers, a technician with a video camera, an orderly, and a hospital social worker who specializes in working with women who have been raped. We all crowd into her room. To my amazement, they accept my presence as reasonable and, even, welcome. I spend a few minutes with Martha, my mouth close to her ear as I whisper a prayer. She does not look at me.

The social worker then asks everyone else except the D.A. and video technician to leave to protect Martha's privacy. A short while later she comes out of the room to say that Martha has been unable to testify. Her responses are vague. She wants to sleep.

"We'll have to try again tomorrow," the D.A. says.

When her son and I are alone, I ask him, "Is this the last thing you want your mother to do in her life? To have to tell this story to strangers?"

He shakes his head. But if she cannot do the deposition the next day, then it is possible the rapist will go free. The D.A. desperately wants to get him. "This guy is scum," she tells me and then uses a stronger word. We all agree.

The next day Martha's son says that he has decided not to push for the deposition. He

. . . . . .

knows she does not have the strength. She is depressed, not responsive to either one of us. Pinned to her hospital gown is a picture of the Virgin Mary. Although she is a Catholic, and she knows I am not, I give her Communion and last rites. In two days, she dies suddenly.

The last words she and I exchange are about Hawaii. I ask her to tell me about her life there the next time I see her. She smiles, perhaps at the memory of being happy somewhere else.

. . . . . .

22
. . . . . .

MY APARTMENT is twenty-seven floors above the street. The view from my living room is arresting: a long stretch of the Hudson River to the George Washington Bridge, the tower of Riverside Church, the Cathedral of St. John the Divine. I like to watch storms gathering over New Jersey boil into Manhattan, especially when there is lightening. Up here is like living on a mountain.

But the street noises rise.

A woman on the sidewalk in front of the bank across Broadway is shouting, "Help me! Somebody please help me!" Her voice is deep, loud, piercing. It is like a solid projectile, blowing people away. Everyone who passes her is horrified. You can see it in their faces. One man in a cowboy hat stops. She is immediately in his face. "I need money for my baby! She needs food and diapers. Help me!" From where I am standing, I cannot hear his reply, but suddenly she falls to her knees, raises clasped hands: "Help me!" When he gives her a coin, she looks at it in the palm of her hand and says, "That's not enough!" He walks by. She follows him, shouting, "Help me!"

One night, sitting on the couch listening to Bach's *Unaccompanied Cello Suites*, I hear her: "Help me! Somebody please help me!" At first, I do not recognize the voice, only the cry for help. I go to the window and look down. I see her pursuing a couple. Then, she spots someone across the street and goes after him. Her voice thuds against the building walls.

Another day she follows a man into the bank while I am in there getting cash. Suddenly the room is filled with her voice. It is an annoying voice, rude and invasive. No one believes that she has a child who needs food. Her teeth are large, strong in a slight body, her mouth a gaping hole of agony. The man she has followed is probably in his thirties, well dressed. He

. . . . . .

turns on her. "Get out of here! You don't belong here. Get out." He steps toward her, menacing. She backs out the door. I hear people say, "Good for you," as if he has committed an act of bravery. Ashamed by my silence, I take my money and leave.

I hear her enter the subway car, her voice like the judgment of God. "Someone help me!" Everyone looks away. She works her way toward me and stops. "Help me!" She looks past me to the next person, not asking me for anything. Her cry for help is generic.

"Where do you live?" I ask her.

Suddenly, she sees me. "What?"

"Where do you live?"

She tells me. "Near the bank," I say. She nods. "You meet me in front of the bank tomorrow morning at eight, and I'll buy food for you."

My words make no sense to her. The "help me" tape begins to run again in her head. "Help me! I need food."

"I'll buy you food."

"No, that's not enough. I need money."

She does not move. "Tomorrow, in front of the bank," I say.

The next morning she is not there. I hang around for fifteen minutes before going on to work.

A few days later, she is back on the corner, haranguing passersby who, like me, do not know what to do with her or for her.

But we can do no miracles here.

. . . . . .

23

THE FIRST SUNDAY I visited St. Clement's Church in Manhattan, where I am now a deacon, I was startled early in the service to hear a dog's whine. Surely not, I thought, looking discreetly behind me. There was an answering whine from the other side of the room. Two dogs! I saw one of them and soon located the other. They were with their owners, on leashes, and for the remainder of the service were quiet and well behaved. I have since gotten to know both of them, Tiger and Molly. They are Sunday regulars.

At first I was not sure what to make of dogs in church. People formed a circle around the altar for Communion at St. Clement's, and when the dogs joined the circle, I said to myself, "If the priest gives them Communion, I'm out of here." They did not receive.

I am still uncertain about the presence of dogs or other animals on a regular basis. Once a year, we typically rejoice in creation by bringing all sorts of animals into the church for blessing on the Feast of St. Francis. The Cathedral of St. John the Divine features an elephant in the procession on that day (and a deacon with a shovel!), but we enjoy this feast because it is unusual.

If everyone brought animals to church on Sundays, I suspect that the practice would quickly be ended. They would no longer be thought of as cute. They would be seen as a nuisance, a distraction, a source of conflict. Some prefer cats and would perhaps want to bring them to church as well. How much cat-and-dog havoc could we stand in the pews? Similar potential for chaos resides in mixing cats and birds.

Even parrots, frequently seen riding peacefully on the shoulders of New Yorkers, are not always benign. A Presbyterian pastor I know tells me about a time when she was visiting a dying man in his home. As she prayed for him, his parrot began to screech, "Go to hell. Go to hell!" Not everyone loves animals. Not everyone loves people either, but in general we feel we ought to *try*.

Do animals have souls? I would not say it that way. All creation is filled with God's Spirit in full measure. Humans do not possess a better Spirit, but we are able to name the Spirit. We are conscious of its presence. Being with Molly and Tiger reminds us of the creative power of the Spirit they cannot name but embody. We cannot understand how they experience the Spirit, but we can sense that the expression of life in them is as powerful as it is in us. Some imagine that the spiritual life of animals is like that we encounter in Zen meditation: the still presence of the ineffable. In that sense, they suggest how we might empty ourselves in prayer.

But they also simply tell us that we are like them. We inhabit the same kingdom of instinct and need.

One hot Sunday we moved our service to the parish hall which, unlike the main church, is air-conditioned. In the smaller space, we were closer together and gathered in a circle. I preached from the center, which allowed me to talk more directly to individuals. At one point, telling a story about an argument I overheard on the street, during which a well-dressed man was physically threatening a woman, I strode toward Tiger's owner shouting in anger. Tiger jumped up and began to bark, straining against the leash.

24
· · · · · ·

DRIVING UP THE HILL to my parents' house I lose control on the ice-covered driveway and slide into the lawn. Suddenly, I am a fifty-five-year-old adolescent. I get out to walk and instantly fall, banging knee and elbow. The bag of groceries splits but nothing breaks. I crawl over the patch of ice and limp to the garage. My father stands there, leaning on his walker. "Are you stuck?"

We have been iced in for two days. Cabin fever has set in. "Yes," I answer evenly.

"Can't you rock it out?"

I go inside. He follows me. We have lunch, during which we talk about what to do. I argue that we should leave the Cadillac where it is. No one will be coming up the drive. We are not going out again. The ice will melt. We clean up the dishes. Dad takes his nap.

My father's life is measured by the automobiles he has owned. Periods of our family life are also defined by cars. There is the year we own the two-toned Chevy (my personal favorite); the age of the Hillman Husky—an anomaly that confirms my father's disdain for foreign makes; the time of the Corvair, which I wreck on Memorial Bridge during rush hour on my way to do research in the Library of Congress when I am a senior in High School (hit a taxi, breaking out both headlights, and then drive on to the library, forgetting that when I come out it will be dark); the blue station wagon in which my first real girlfriend and I first French-kissed after watching *A Summer Place*. Then following his retirement to Madison, Virginia, come the golden years of the Cadillacs (confirming the man my father wanted to be) and the pickup trucks (reclaiming the inner "good ol' boy" from Arizona). The Chrysler convertible that sits in the garage and is seldom started, much less driven, is an oddity, a last gasp of open road and blowing hair when his hair is most-

· · · · · ·

ly gone, bought for him by my mother. I don't expect him ever to sell it or give it away, even though all four of his grandsons covet it. I imagine that his will contains a clause requiring that it be buried with him. Then my father sells the last of the pickups—I think there were three—and stops driving. He has no choice. Parkinson's has weakened him severely. His reflexes are slow. Ironically, my mother has the accidents during the year he stops driving.

I help him dress when he wakes from his nap. Looking through the bedroom window at the immobile car, he says softly, "That's what's so bad about this."

"Parkinson's?"

He nods in the slightly off-balance way he has, head tilted left and down. "Not being able to drive any more."

He misses it. He does not read or listen to music. He never has. He has played golf, bowled, driven cars. Now he can do none of those things.

He heads toward the garage. "Where are you going?" I ask.

"To move the Cadillac," he says.

"Leave it there," mom says.

He keeps going, the wheels of the walker squeaking. I follow him to the garage door. He opens it and looks out at the stuck car. Between us and the car is what he always calls a "glare" of ice.

"You can't go out there," I say. "You'll fall and hurt yourself. I fell."

"No I won't." He starts to push the wheels of the walker to the top step. I put my hand on his shoulder and restrain him.

"You're not going out there. We'll call a tow truck if you want it moved."

He turns on me quickly, with a look I remember from my childhood. "Don't you preach to me," he shouts. Then he turns and pushes his walker back down the hall, saying

· · · · · ·

to mom as he goes by, "After eighty years I guess I just haven't learned anything. I'm good for nothing."

I suddenly recall a photograph of me with my father and mother: I am beginning to walk and he is just back from the war. They are standing in the snow on Mount Lemmon, near Tucson. He wears a short-sleeved shirt. Near them is a black car. It might be the Ford sedan he bought after the war. He holds my arms as if to steady me but is looking over at the car, smiling. It is the one he always says he should have kept.

. . . . .

25
. . . . .

BECAUSE I LIKE TO TALK, I used to love lunch meetings. Years of working as a publisher with an expense account and a taste for good food made lunch a favorite time of day. In the past ten years, however, I have not had as many opportunities to "do lunch," mainly because I no longer have an expense account, but I found myself at lunch not too long ago in one of those New York university clubs frequented by the influential. There were four of us around the table—my boss at *Cross Currents*, a religion reporter from one of New York's major newspapers, and a writer who had written an interesting book about faith seekers at the end of the millennium.

We have gathered to do some professional networking. There is no real agenda. The writer had returned to the Episcopal Church but at the same time was experimenting with Zen; she also frequented a synagogue on the Upper West Side that is the center of a Jewish spirituality movement that is both smart and somewhat charismatic. (Her husband is a Jew.) The reporter described herself as "secular," although she is from a Jewish household. My boss and I are ordained, he in the Presbyterian Church. We are all New Age intellectuals, open to just about any permutation in the religious gene pool.

Following some small talk, the reporter suggested, "All religion is based in consumerism. Religious institutions are merely competing for market share."

"It's really a recent phenomenon," I reply, "a product of advertising."

"Religion has always been a commodity." Her look suggested to me that she was already bored with religion as a topic of conversation. I wondered why she became a religion reporter and was not doing sports.

"Religion *is* big business," my boss agreed. In his estimation, the problem is that the

. . . . . .

mainline denominations are losing market share to the Evangelicals and the Community Church Movement (places such as Willow Creek in South Barrington, Illinois, which attracts 17,000 people to weekend services), not to mention New Age spirituality.

"Not everyone thinks that the decline of the mainline is a problem," the writer said. "I don't miss it."

At about this point in the conversation, I wondered how faith entered into the equation. What does it mean that I have *faith*? I suspected that the question would not make sense to the journalist. I wondered if the writer thought of herself as faithful.

We covered the other contemporary religious issue bases: the influence of the Internet on the practice of religion; homosexuality and the Church; the increasing number of Eastern religious groups in cities; the growth of Islam among African Americans. We agreed that the young have left the Church but that they might come back, as the Boomers did, when they have children.

Talking about religion is like talking about politics. Nothing happens.

"Contemporary religion," I said, unable to stop myself, "is less religion than a system of psychological supports." I heard myself and thought I was being extremely bright. "Religious organizations are surviving by giving people what they think they need in small groups organized around special interests. Religion should be something quite different."

Religion, I thought, is about faith, but I did not say that. One does not give testimony in the Princeton Club.

The survival of traditional religion matters to those of us who are part of the established Church, but I am willing to accept that the form of religion will certainly change, perhaps even in my lifetime. What, however, will we believe? Who is God for us in the contemporary world? Do the formulations of faith in the traditional Church bind or liberate us? Those are the questions, not the survival of the Church, that ought to absorb our interest.

· · · · · ·

I had been neglecting my lunch and began to eat my Nicoise salad, briefly tuning out a conversation that was all too familiar. I had been having this discussion, or ones just like it, for thirty years, beginning with my early days as an editor in Washington, D.C., when I did daily "important" lunches with authors. (I did not believe in anything back then but a restaurant called Bixby's Warehouse.)

I was brought back to the present when the writer observed, "I'm not sure I can do intercessory prayer anymore."

There was a sense of general agreement among the three of them. "How," my boss wondered, "can you explain a God who intervenes only because someone asks?"

The question of intercessory prayer goes right to the heart of what we mean by a community of faith. So many of our cultural assumptions about religion are based on the assumption that God endorses private purpose. The average person might think that praying for others should produce results that he or she can see. Otherwise, why do it? Going to church should be personally beneficial. Worship should serve personal needs and the needs of friends and relatives.

In fact, faith does not serve my needs. Spiritual practice does not produce results in the way that ideas, theories, and plans over lunch might produce results. Faith does not depend on results. If the Church only meets my needs, I am less likely to be there for others. And I am less likely to recognize the God who is always there for me.

The writer said, "But lately I've been thinking about people who really do intercede for others. I want to write my next book about contemporary saints, the ones who have given themselves away completely. Do you know any?"

I don't think I can do lunch anymore.

. . . . . .

26
· · · · ·

ONE MORNING ON FORTY-SECOND STREET in Manhattan, I see a woman in line to board a bus punch the woman behind her. Her move is quick and practiced. This is not the first person she has slugged. She shouts, "You stop pushing me!" A group of tourists pauses to take pictures, delighted to see New York in action. Others in the bus line step away. The one who is attacked, smaller and older, seems stunned by what has happened. But when her assailant turns her back, she begins pounding her shoulders with glancing and ineffectual blows of rage.

It surprises me that most of us get through the day without being injured or injuring each other. Lately, when someone pushes by me to take the last subway seat or jumps to the front of the line at the coffee shop, I have been saying, "Please, I want you to be first." The response is usually a murderous stare.

Please, I want you to be first. The attitude is a hard one to grasp. (I do it out of anger as a rule and therefore it cannot be counted to me as righteousness.) John the Baptist understands the implications of stepping aside for someone else. He is as pure a servant minister as anyone in the New Testament. Suddenly, in the crowds along the Jordan River, he sees Jesus and *knows*. Out of the chaos comes this still point of light, and he sees it. I imagine that the scene freezes for John. Everyone but Jesus stops moving. Imagine being so tuned to creation that—as you are working, even as you are absorbed in your own life, as John is—you sense the arrival of God. A door opens and there, in the light: look!

It is what the prophet does, shows us the reality. Prophets are not just the ones who shout, although John apparently was a shouter: the voice of one crying in the wilderness. He is the last of the prophets of Israel, standing in the Jordan at the door to the Promised Land, telling

· · · · · ·

all who will listen, "you are children of the snake." They flock to his abuse, even the ruling classes who should know better. What do they think he is going to say? Jesus later asks the same questions: What do you go to the prophet to hear? What do you want to know?

The kingdom of heaven crashes like thunder into a cloudless day. The crowd parts like the waters of the Red Sea. John points. Heads turn. This is a moment when sacred time enters human space. Does anyone else see anything, or is it only John, only the one pointing? John says that this is the one greater than he, the one whose sandals he is unworthy to fasten, the one he has been talking about. The genuine prophet always points beyond the self. John's work is finished—*he* is finished—the moment this one steps out of the crowd and asks to be washed. John replies, "No. It's the other way around. You wash me. I am not worthy."

He is mistaken.

When we wash someone else, we give them honor. We acknowledge the holiness of their flesh, even as John recognizes holy flesh in Jesus. When our children are young, we wash them. It is often a time of laughter, splashing in the bath. When our parents grow old, sometimes we wash them too, when they are too sick or feeble to care for themselves. This is another kind of reverence, caring for those who brought us into the world, honoring their flesh.

When my father had seizures at few years ago, I spent some time with my mother taking care of him. Together we washed him. He is a man who hates to give up control, but he put up with our soaping his body, making a joke of it. "Vi," he said, "you wash the top part as far down as possible. Ken, you wash up as far as possible. And," he grinned, "I'll wash possible."

I remember the surprise of the smoothness of his skin.

It is a moment, this washing of one another, in which we must decrease while the other, the one we wash, increases. Jesus teaches the lesson explicitly on Maundy Thursday, when he insists on washing the disciples' feet. "See what I your Lord have done for you. I have given you an example."

The crowds on the highway, the throngs in the subway, are all those Jesus invites us to wash. Among them he is also walking. The crowd is threatening. People push us aside on their way somewhere else. The moment can be terrifying when we are engulfed by strangers. Stuck in traffic, we have nowhere to go. The subway doors close us in with people filled with resentment, hundreds of thousands of them, each the hidden presence of God. When all I am thinking about is my own journey home, I will not see the one who is among them. But it is a fearsome thing to look too closely, for when God emerges in the crowd, time stops, as it does for John. After that I must decrease.

Salvation is like that. It's not about me.

27
. . . . . .

THE FIRST PEOPLE Jesus calls to be his disciples are busy at the time. They are doing what they normally do—mending nets, collecting taxes, eating. They are not expecting anything out of the ordinary. It is the normal way to live, assuming the ordinary. In fact, we count on the ordinary. And yet, somehow, Jesus calls them in a way that breaks through the normal routine. His voice changes everything. They look up from what they are doing. They stop what they are doing.

That is what it means to be on call in the work world. As a volunteer chaplain at St. Luke's Hospital in Manhattan, I am on call during the weekends. I carry a beeper, which often goes off at inconvenient times. On one occasion, I am standing in line to buy movie tickets. I have been sound asleep. When the beeper goes off, I call the hospital and, usually, have to go there to visit someone who is sick or dying or, even, dead. The beeper is annoying. It calls me to go where I may not want to go.

One Sunday evening, the beeper sounds while I am eating dinner. I am tired, as I often am at the end of the day on Sunday. There is nothing planned for the evening, and I am looking forward to doing exactly nothing. The call is from the emergency room—not a good sign. A woman has been raped. She wants to see the chaplain. Although I have no training in counseling rape victims, I have to go. There is no one else.

It is raining. There are no taxis. The subway line is closed for weekend repairs. I walk the fifteen blocks to the hospital. Along the way, I pray that Jesus will come along with me, that I will not have to do this work alone. By the time I reach St. Luke's, I feel that my prayer has been answered.

It is a typical weekend in the emergency room—crowded, frenzied. People moan with

. . . . . .

pain. The woman who has been raped begins to cry when I walk into the cubicle. She seizes my hands. I sit down by her. She looks at me with fear and starts to tell me her story. She is nearly incoherent. I ask her to stop for a moment.

"Wait," I say. "Jesus is here with us. Let's take a moment to welcome him."

"He's here?" She asks me.

Immediately, she calms down. Her face softens. She says she is angry. "Is it OK to be angry?" She wants to know.

"Yes," I reply. "You can be angry. You have a right to be angry."

And then I tell her to read some of the psalms of rage, the ones we usually skip, the parts about smashing our enemies until their blood runs on the ground. She knows those psalms. She is relieved that I give her permission to pray them.

"God is with you even in your pain and your anger," I assure her.

We talk awhile longer, but in a sense my bringing God to her in Jesus and in the psalms is all that I can do. I am not being asked to counsel her or to pretend to have expertise that I do not have. I have been called to do one thing and have done it.

. . . . .

28
· · · · · ·

ONE SIGN READS, "Tampa, Magic Kingdom"; the other, "Orlando, Downtown Disney." Those are the choices. Although I feel drawn to Magic Kingdom, my meeting is in Downtown Disney. I take the right fork in the road and eventually come to the Disney World Dolphin Hotel. I recognize it right away by the grinning blue dolphin perched on its chin beyond the exit ramp.

That night, I walk along the waterway between the hotel and Epcot Center. It looks a bit like Venice but a Venice that is odorless, denatured, unreal. I think about *The Truman Show*, the movie in which Jim Carrey's character lives a "perfect" life until he begins to realize that the world around him is staged and the people in his life are scripted. Truman rejects a show of life that refuses death. He runs away from Downtown Disney toward reality.

While I was away on this trip to Orlando, a member of my parish died. Before I left, his doctor told me that he would not last much longer. I took Communion to him and administered last rites. Abraham had been in and out of the hospital for several months. His lung cancer was diagnosed in the summer, but treatment was complicated by his being HIV positive. Although we had known each other for a couple of years, during his illness we became close. Because his relatives, including his children, had been estranged from him, I became his family.

When I entered the room, he raised his arms to hug me, as he always did. The motion made me think of a child asking a parent to pick him up, even though we were the same age. We talked for a while, although it was difficult for him because he wore an oxygen mask. His lungs were filled with fluid. When he tried to speak, his words were garbled by the gurgling in his throat.

· · · · · ·

I said, "Abraham, I want to give you Communion." He nodded. I usually brought him Communion. "And also what we call last rites. I'm going away for a few days. And you might not live until I come back. So I want us to pray together. I may not see you again."

He stared blankly at me. We had talked before about his death, but Abraham had had trouble in his life facing truth, and confronting this approaching death was no easier. Recognition came into his eyes, however, as I said the Lord's Prayer and the Prayer of Confession. I assured him of God's forgiveness for his sins, touched his forehead with the Communion wafer, and then read the "Litany at the Time of Death." I did this for him as a deacon in the Church and also with him as a friend.

We looked together at the reality of life's inevitable end and, at the same time, the truth of our lives together in the communion of saints. We are each called to look suffering in the face—in our own faces, in the faces of others. If we deny our own suffering and pain, then we will fail to see it in those who need our care. When I placed my hands on his head and prayed that "he may rest with all your saints in the eternal habitations," I wanted him to know that he would not be alone in this death even after I left.

We embraced and said, as we always did when we parted, "I love you."

Abraham died in a reality he had avoided most of his life. And we were in it together. Downtown Disney is not the end of our journey.

29

. . . . . .

WHEN THE TELEPHONE RANG on Saturday night, I answered it and heard my mother's voice. She began to cry. For two days, she had been struggling to cope with my father's insomnia. He had been hallucinating. I could hear the fear in her voice. She asked if I could be available to come down if things got worse. I decided to go down to Madison, Virginia, where they live in retirement first thing Sunday morning. Things were already bad enough.

My mother is not one to ask directly for help. She has a strong sense of boundaries and is reluctant to impose on others. My father has Parkinson's Disease and, at eighty-one, is frail and forgetful. She has chosen to care for him at home. The house is on a hillside near the Blue Ridge Mountains, and I can appreciate their not wanting to move. The place is beautiful.

My sisters and I worry about that decision because of the stress it places on her. Although she is in good health, she has some arthritis and back pain. She is nearly eighty. Because I live in New York City, I do not own a car. My normal transportation to Madison is the Peter Pan Greyhound Bus, which drops me off in Culpeper, Virginia, at a Texaco station I call the Gas 'n' Go. Mother picked me up at about four in the afternoon and on the way home told me about what had been happening. At one point she said that she heard her mother's voice when she was desperately awake with worry tell her: "Don't be afraid. You go to sleep. I'll take care of him."

The first night I am here, however, is actually a good one. He has stopped hallucinating. She is more rested, less tense. I am still glad I have come.

He is not seeing little green men. His hallucinations are drawn from his normal life. They return on Monday morning as I am eating breakfast with him. He says that he called his sis-

. . . . . .

ter this morning in Illinois. I have been with him and know he did not call her or anyone. He says he hears someone knocking at the door and declares that it is the man up the road who used to pick him up on Mondays to have breakfast with the guys down at the MacDonald's. There is no knocking. He wonders if my kids, who have not been here since Christmas, took the extra remote control from his bedroom while he was asleep.

He is creating a narrative based on a reality he knows.

I have work to do, appointments to cancel. This unexpected trip has disrupted my life. But I cannot imagine any other response, even though both of my parents slept soundly last night and this morning my father seems to be fine, despite his active imagination. Sitting with him on the deck in the warm morning sun, I can imagine a time when he will not know who I am and will have only confused stories in his head—confused but nonetheless his.

There are times in prayer, especially during extended meditation, when I lose focus and my mind is suddenly flooded with dream-like images, but not like dreams, as if there is a story parallel to my own that is just waiting to break in. If I let go for even a moment, the other story is there, like a movie in progress. What is strange about it is that the other story contains pieces of my own. I recognize what is going on even though it makes no sense. I want to go into this other story but yank myself back to my meditation. Struggle to stay in the moment.

I wonder if death is like this: the gradual giving in to this parallel story that is somehow also ours.

My father looks up abruptly. "Who's that?" He points at the empty deck bright with sunlight.

· · · · · ·

30

I TAKE MY PARENTS' DOG Missy for a walk in the afternoon. We go down the hill, following the road through the woods and see no one else. There are six houses along the way, but it is Monday and people are working. At the bottom of the hill, we follow a dirt trail that leads to a farm pond I have not seen before. It looks new. Small sunfish are poking around the neat edges. We walk back.

Along the way I find myself thinking about the new biography of Martin Luther I have been reading. People in his day were terrified of the forest—as the Grimm fairy tales make amply clear. Luther's conversion experience, which sent him into a monastery, occurred in a thunderstorm in the woods. These woods in Virginia are tame, filled with sun. At night they are spooky, to be sure, but not filled, as Luther's were, with demons. I am struck by the fact that Luther walked when he wanted to go somewhere (or hitched a ride on a passing cart). He and others in the past thought nothing of walking substantial distances to go somewhere, taking days to do it.

Jesus also walked a lot. Mendicant friars, such as the Franciscans and Dominicans, got out of their monasteries to do ministry on the road, depending on those they met for their support. Luther hated them. He walked to get somewhere. The Mendicants just walked around. Jesus just walked too, even when he was going to the next town. He was willing to stop along the way, turn off in a new direction if he was needed.

In Manhattan I walk a couple of miles every day, usually going somewhere in a hurry. Today, walking Missy in Virginia, I am not going anywhere. I put one foot in front of the other deliberately, trying to feel the earth under it, pushing off as if a step means something. There is a walking like this in Zen known as *kin hin*, which is a form of meditation or mindfulness. I am trying to walk mindfully through the woods, conscious of my breathing. My head fills with light. I am trying to be completely open.

Walking like this is prayer, even when there is no sound in my head. But after a while, I am saying to myself what is known as the Jesus Prayer, "Lord Jesus Christ, have mercy on me," coordinating each syllable with a step in an even rhythm. The prayer is Russian Orthodox, the walk is Zen, the mind is Luther, the temple is the woods.

When I stop moving because Missy has found something to sniff in the leaves, I continue to say the prayer in the rhythm of my walking so that when I begin again my body resumes the flow of my internal motion. There is no point to this prayer except the praying itself, as the walk has no destination. It is simply the walk, simply the prayer. I am an empty place for the Spirit.

I think about what it might be like to walk this way in New York, to hold my internal motion even when the subway doors are about to close or the crossing light is about to change. This kind of walking recognizes the Spirit in a place. Luther knew the spirits, mostly the demonic spirits, it seems. Jesus knew them too, both good and evil. Because he walked purposefully, he sensed what was going on around him, as he did, for example, when the woman with the flow of blood touched him in the crowd. Even though he was on the way to bring a young girl from death into life, Jesus did not sacrifice anyone to urgency.

Every journey is its own reality. The Spirit is where we are in the present, not somewhere else.

. . . . .

31

THE POLICE RADIO in my parents' kitchen is always on, scanning for emergencies. Out here in the country, it is one of the ways we know what is happening. The voice crackles, and I think at first someone in the other room is speaking.

"All units, auto accident on 29 South at Brandy."

I know exactly where that is, Brandy Station, site of a Civil War battle but for me one of the constant landmarks of my life. I passed it often on trips north or south to Lynchburg, when I was in school there, and now to Madison, where my parents live. There is not much to Brandy Station—principally an old church building that after many years of being empty is now something modern like an outlet store. When I was in college, we passed right through the intersection that is Brandy. Now, a highway passes it by. One has to choose to go to Brandy.

"Be passersby," Jesus says in the Gospel of Thomas. But he does not mean "go around." He means "go right through the middle of things."

Someone is injured at Brandy Station. All units are asked to respond. They have to go. The rest of us, those who are listening to the scanner, learn nothing more. We have to imagine the rest or remember the stories we have heard. At lunch today, over at the country club, I met a man whose son is still in serious condition following an accident a month ago. Traveling the wrong way, drunk or confused, the driver of the pickup truck that hit him died.

"All units respond."

Some of the people who go are volunteers. I imagine them as they leap up from what they are doing—at a desk or in a ditch—and drive away with blue lights flashing on the dashboard. An hour later they are back at work, having responded. Perhaps they say nothing about where they've been. It is routine. The rest of us know nothing more than "accident at Brandy" and perhaps "personal injury." There is only the next announcement about the next emergency: "Brush fire out of control at Pratt's."

There is danger everywhere. Sometimes it seems to target us. My friend Kathy went to Asia last week, where she is traveling while I visit my parents. Earlier this week in Korea, her flight was troubled by a typhoon, although not a large one. A few days later a massive earthquake in Taiwan took 2,000 lives, maybe more. By then she was in the Philippines, but the paper said there might be a tsunami from the earthquake. This morning, she told me that another typhoon was bearing down on Japan, and she might not be able to make her scheduled connection.

The police radio in Madison reports that someone has fallen off of a roof near Ruckersville, six miles down the road. The Madison Rescue Squad knows nothing of Kathy's plight. But in Fairfax, ninety minutes up the road, an elite emergency team is flying off to Taiwan to help rescue victims of the quake. A month ago they were in Turkey after a disaster in which even more were killed.

These are passersby, these units that travel to Ruckersville and Taiwan. They come and do their work and then they go, expecting nothing. It is work of almost Gospel purity, to be summoned, go, and then go back to whatever you were doing as if nothing had happened. This passing by is not like the passing by of those who passed the injured man in the parable of the Samaritan. Those who ignored him had an agenda. The injured man was unclean or of the wrong ethnic group. He represented politics. The passersby that Jesus spoke about responded not to politics but to need. They were not among the injured as themselves or as heroes. Their behavior is normal in the kingdom.

This is one of the meanings of the word "selfless."

. . . . .

32
. . . . . .

"Lenora said it was sad the children don't know God. 'Most of them are going to die, and are going to go to hell,' she said."

Lenora is sixteen. I read her comment in this morning's *Eagle*, the weekly newspaper published in Madison, my parents' hometown. Along with eight other young people from the Thoroughfare Baptist Church, Lenora recently spent five weeks as a missionary among the Yuqui, one of the indigenous peoples of Bolivia. Sponsored by New Tribes Mission, which specializes in evangelizing "unreached tribes," the young people were learning what it is like to be missionaries.

When I first came to New York, I was also a missionary. Portraying St. Francis, I went through the subway with an artificial bird's nest filled with coins, offering people money instead of begging them for it. I also did this on the street. I walked up to people and held out the bird's nest to them. "Would you like some money," I asked. "It's free," I said. Most people quickly backed away. They wanted nothing to do with me. One mother was indignant when I offered money to her son, who was clearly tempted. It was obvious that I was a danger to him in some way she could not identify. At the time, I was working on a one-man show in which I was to be St. Francis, and I wanted to feel his strangeness in my own body. Giving money away in New York seemed like the sort of thing Francis would do. But I did not plan to do it. One day, the impulse just seized me. Walking through the subway car with that bird's nest in my hand made me understand Francis as the performance poet I imagine he was. He acted out the Gospel shamelessly. (As he put it, "Preach the Gospel constantly. Use words if you have to.")

It was difficult giving money away, especially to people with money. The poor had no

. . . . . .

trouble taking what I offered, although some were concerned that I had a new racket that would end up taking money from them. Panhandlers wanted nothing to do with me. They have their established routes, their routines, their clientele. Even though I was giving money away, I looked like them. I was competition on their turf.

A good missionary needs a message, as Lenora knows. My message went something like this:

> Good morning. The kingdom of God is like a man who went onto the subway trains and gave money to others from a begging bowl. He gave money to rich and poor alike, to the well-dressed and the naked. There were no strings attached. Those who wanted money were free to take it. This is the meaning of the parable. God created you and loves you. You have nothing to worry about. Everything is going to be all right. God loves you exactly as you are, with all of your faults. There is nothing you can do to earn God's grace. It has already been given to you. Give thanks for your life.

My friends were embarrassed when I did this in their presence. They also worried that I would be injured, that someone would attack me for giving away money.

"But why," I wanted to know, "would someone attack me for giving away money?"

"Because," my friend Kathy told me, "it scares them. They can understand someone preaching about damnation. They can understand it because they have heard it before, and they don't believe it. But when you give them something for nothing and tell them that God is like that, they get nervous. It makes them angry."

No missionary preaching love is safe. Only those who preach hell and damnation can get away with it. The prophets in the Hebrew scriptures may have preached God's anger, but it feels to me like the anger of a lover. They did the hard work of saving people. It is easy to send someone to hell. Generosity will get you thrown out of the subway.

. . . .

33

THE PHILOSOPHER'S PATH parallels an old canal for three miles along the base of the mountains in the eastern suburbs of Kyoto, Japan. It is a popular place for walkers, joggers, and tourists. The neighborhood is picturesque and affluent. There are cafes, small curio and souvenir shops, new and renovated houses. I have read about the Path in Kyoto guide books and want to walk it—not for the shops but for the Buddhist temples along the way. Since I am in Japan, and especially in Kyoto, as a pilgrim tourist, I set out to find the Path on a Saturday afternoon in winter. It has become for me the heart of this pilgrimage. I do not yet know why.

The Path is not easy to find, even though it is famous. Once found, it is suspiciously neat, too perfect in every way. Midway in my journey, I sit in a coffee shop overlooking the Path and sip cappuccino while listening to Mozart. This is not exactly Pilgrim's Progress, although the temptation to stay here for the afternoon is real enough. Not far from the coffee shop, I walk up a small hill to a Buddhist temple, Honen-in, tucked into the woods. It is one of two temples I want to visit along the Path, although neither is my destination. The truth is I have no destination.

There are a few times in our lives when we can enter into such states, when we are separated from the ordinary not only physically but emotionally. These are states of emptiness, in which whatever comes along is perfect. Lent can be like that. The Lenten journey takes place in the emptiness we picture as a desert, which is our destination even as we travel through it. This emptiness is not a vehicle by which we accomplish something. It is itself. (Jesus empties himself so that we can enter his emptiness. That is what it means, I think, to leave everything and follow him. It is in that sense that he is way, truth, and life. The way is the end.)

As I walk up the hill toward Honen-in, I begin to feel like the diminutive hermit in the typical Japanese scroll painting, a speck in the overwhelming landscape. One would have to look carefully to find me here. I ascend the stone steps from the road, along which sports cars covered in protective nylon are parked. The approach to Honen-in is paved in cobblestone. On the ridge above is a Buddhist cemetery. I can see the gardener moving among the memorial markers. The winter day is warm. Sunlight graces the pines.

There is a kind of Zen meditation that is done while walking. Every step is intentional. The body's motion frees the mind: as we pass through the landscape so do our thoughts pass through us. I feel I have stepped into this zone in which my walking is all that there is. I come and go as a thought, a memory, a snatch of song.

In this temple there is an altar before which the monks place, every morning at 4:30, a dozen chrysanthemum blossoms, representing a pantheon of bodhisattvas (enlightened beings—saints—who choose to remain caught in time to help the rest of us instead of retiring in nirvana). I want to see this altar, which is all I know about Honen-in. Perhaps I am looking for the traditional beauty of flowers on an altar, the scent of incense, the exotic.

From the top of the steps at the entrance to the temple grounds, I look down on two rectangular mounds of dirt flanking the walk that leads to the gardens. A monk in a blue robe is carving out of the top of one of the mounds sinuous ridges that might be paths or mountains, his attention fixed on smoothing the surface of the mound. At first I see him from a great distance. He is a Buddhist monk in Japan; I am a Christian from the United States touring temples, with a camera around my neck. My home is Manhattan. His home is this tranquility.

· · · · · ·

So much of my life suddenly feels like the bullet train between Tokyo and Kyoto—all speed in a landscape cluttered with the debris of the modern. The train seems to be running away from something, perhaps from everything, aggressively charging into anything new, the used landscapes eaten by ego. Although I cannot imagine this monk's life—and probably would not like living it—I know this space. It feels like holy ground, a place where one takes off shoes because God is palpable, not—as in most of Japan—because custom demands it.

I know that I am at the edge of the desert, where the spirits dwell, and that I have come to Japan to be with this monk carving the earth. God has created us for the same emptiness. The monk looks at me, as I descend the steps, and returns to his work.

When Jesus goes into the desert, he is called to this emptiness of reality. He lets go, carving away from himself the extraneous matter that obscures the way. It is what we do as well in Lent, however painfully. The emptiness we seek is a letting go, a taking away, so that the Christ can be revealed as our journey, even as the monk in Honen-in reveals his path, and mine, as a mound of dirt.

Walking through the monastery's small garden, I am aware of the newness of everything, even the carp in the pond. The paths disclose themselves as I come to them, as they seldom do in those transitions in ordinary time when I cannot be sure where to go and what to do. God shows the way, but only if I am paying attention in my daily life, if I see each moment as indebted to the Spirit. The dirt mounds the monks carve at Honen-in are only dirt mounds, and then they are icons of presence.

34
. . . . . .

THE WOOD RIVER'S water is the color of cedar. It flows through the Arcadia Wildlife Management Area in Rhode Island. There are trout in it, and for years I have fished the river in the summer. This year I leave my campsite before dawn; by 6 A.M. I am on the river's bank looking down into a deep, still pool. It is a different river from a year before, when heavy rains made it almost unfishable. On that trip, I caught one trout, stepped in a deep hole, nearly broke my leg. But this year there is a drought. The river is low and clear.

There are no other cars in the dirt lot where anglers park, but the woods are alive with bird song and the occasional crash of an animal running off when it hears me coming. I step into the river above a bend that I know holds fish, relishing the cold through my waders. The water is fairly deep here. I have room to cast, even though the banks are high and brushy. Staying low, I cross to a small sandbar and kneel. A fish breaks the surface around the bend beneath a low leafy branch. I will have to cast a line under the branch and land a fly near the bank twenty feet away.

The fly I am using is one that has worked for me on the Wood before. It lights on the river, drifts, stutters on the surface when I twitch the line, and is taken in a splashy rise by the fourteen-inch, brown trout. He is extravagantly colored in orange, yellow, lavender, red. Everything stops for this excess. When I release him, he disappears instantly in the clear water.

Before the morning is over, I take two more fish but none as gorgeous or as large as the first. By late morning, the air is hot and still. I do not need to catch more fish. At noon I am back on the road, driving home to New York City. Swept along with the traffic, I think about how remarkable it is to be completely alone for any length of time, to be silent for

. . . .

several hours: alone, but not separated from the net of life that holds everything. It is the difference between loneliness and being alone.

There is an image from Hinduism, Indra's Net, which represents the universe and how its parts relate to the whole. At each intersection of the net's strands there is a polished bead in which all of the rest of the net is reflected. Each part of the net, then, contains the whole. And each bead is separate from the others. Each is, in a sense, alone, even as I am alone in the stream of traffic or the trout is alone in the river. At the same time, there is only one reality, the net completely contained in me and in the fish, each of us wholly contained in God. Indra's Net makes sense to me. It is the way things are.

When I am stalled in traffic on the Cross-Bronx Expressway two hours after leaving the river, I feel that I still contain it and am held by it. This way of being alone invites life and makes revelation possible.

I imagine casting a line into the traffic, drifting the right fly among those who are lonely. I bring one of them to me from a deep part of the river. How surprised we are to see each other.

35

THE INFANT in the emergency room might be sleeping except for the tube in its mouth and the stained sheet. His mother stands weeping at the entrance to the cubicle in bare feet. It is seven o'clock on a Sunday morning in June when I arrive.

Pentecost.

I tell her, "There is nothing worse than this, the death of your child. But you're not alone. Many of us have gone through it and lived."

She looks sharply at me: her eyes ask if I'm lying. "Why did God take him from me?"

"God doesn't take. Death takes all of us. And God loves all of us."

She does not want to leave the baby. Uncomfortable with grief, a friend who is with her wants to go. He is not sure what to do or say. "She'll be OK," he says more than once.

I pray for the baby, my arm around the mother and my hand on the child's cold head. "We give thanks for this child." I make the sign of the cross on his forehead.

After a long silence, I say to the dead child's mother, "You need to say goodbye to him now."

She staggers slightly as she goes to the side of the bed. "Forgive me," she says to him.

Although she has told me a story of what happened, I have no way of knowing the truth. I do not know what there is to forgive, but there is always something left undone at the end of our lives with others, no matter how young the dead. I suspect we always want the departed to forgive us. They have the last word.

The life spirit has gone from this child—and something has died in his mother as well.

It is the opposite of the simple service of Baptism I perform in the same hospital later in the day for a different child, very much alive. I call down the Holy Spirit on one who knows nothing of what is being done for her. I sign her warm forehead with chrism. "You are marked as Christ's own forever," I say. The teenaged mother watches anxiously, while the equally young father takes pictures with a disposable camera. Their daughter is going into foster care after I baptize her. I give them a candle, take a picture of the two of them with the baby. They take one of me holding her.

"God bless you both," I say as I leave.

Through the glass wall I can see them with their baby, looking like any other couple. I am touched by their innocence, their obvious belief that all will be well. They have plans. Soon, when they are older and able to care for the child, they will bring her home. I pray they will.

After I do the Baptism, I take Communion to Alpha, a parishioner who is a retired nurse. Her nine-year-old daughter Tia runs in and out of the room getting ready to go to the park, interrupting the Gospel and our prayers with the details of finding her clothes and getting dressed.

As Tia speeds out the door, Alpha says she has never understood about the Holy Spirit. "But when someone died in the hospital, sometimes I'd see a light go out of them and right through the window. You could see it go, the spirit right out of them. That's the way I think of it."

I give her Communion. The Spirit comes. The Spirit goes. It is like breathing, or a light that goes on and goes off. Nothing is lost.

36

THERE WAS A TIME when I thought I might be called to be a priest. As I discussed my vocation with others, one friend asked me this question: What objects do you see yourself handling? At first the question struck me as odd, but then in my mind I looked at the altar set for the Eucharist. I knew what I wanted to touch—and what she wanted me to see. The quintessential image of the priest is the two hands elevating the host during the Eucharist, handling the body of Christ. In the Roman Catholic Church, the hierarchy of minor to major orders brings one closer to the privilege of touching the body, of consecrating the bread. Although Christians, especially Protestants, have lost some of that sense of awe, we have regained an understanding of Christ's presence for all of us in worship, not only in the hands of the priest.

Nonetheless, the priest elevates the host. A deacon holds the chalice. Deacons handle vessels.

The holiness of touching common things—the sanctification of the ordinary—became clearer to me in Japan, when I realized what happens in the traditional ceremony of tea. The ceremony is highly stylized. It occurs in a place set apart for preparing and serving tea. Particular vessels and implements are used. The host making the tea dresses in a certain, formal way. Each gesture is studied, from the measuring of the tea powder to the lighting of the charcoal and the pouring of the heated water into the bowl. The tea itself is drunk attentively, while kneeling.

There is no religious meaning attached to the ceremony of tea, although it is associated in the minds of many with Zen. It is a ritual that has meaning in the same way meditative practice has meaning. We are brought to be wholly present in the moment, completely focused on our relationship to the tea, vessels, implements, space, and other people. In the ceremony, we become part of the beauty of the event, which exists for its own sake. The meaning is in the thing itself. The ceremony of tea calms the mind and spirit by honoring the dignity of objects and time.

In the Eucharist we take ordinary objects—a cup, a plate, linens, a cruet for water—and treat them with reverence, not only because they will be used to bear the Body and Blood of Christ but because they are in themselves significant in creation. When I set the eucharistic table, I devote my attention to each object. Such attentiveness is not as easy as it might seem. There are constant distractions, even during the Eucharist. My mind wanders. I begin thinking about something someone has said or a problem that I know I will have to deal with later in the day. As in contemplative prayer, I have to bring myself back from each digression to the moment in which I am now living.

This way of being extends from the Eucharist to all of life. It is also a teaching in Zen. Whatever you are doing, do only that. Focus all of your attention on this action, these objects. When you are cooking, cook. When you are washing dishes, wash dishes. I have a tendency to do more than one thing at a time. Most of us do. It is a characteristic of our technological state of being. We call it multitasking. People walk and talk on cellular phones, listen to music through headsets and read, watch television and eat. We think of this as efficiency. But it seems to me a denial of reality. If the real is sacred—and the Incarnation tells us it is—then each object we encounter in the world, and each movement we make, is worthy of our full attention.

37

I AM STANDING with Jesus on the corner of Seventh Avenue and Thirteenth Street at about 6 A.M. It is Good Friday morning. Along with another member of St. Clement's, I have arrested Jesus and taken him away from the courtyard of St. John's in the Village, where we have spent the past several hours re-enacting events surrounding Peter's denial of Jesus. We began what we called "The Real Time Passion" with the Maundy Thursday service and have been awake now for twenty-four hours. The man playing Jesus is wrapped in a brown blanket. There is virtually no one on the street.

I put my hand on Jesus' shoulder. "Promise not to run off?"

He laughs. "This is weird, you know."

We head up the avenue toward General Seminary where, in a couple of hours, we will try Jesus before Pilate. We have left the others behind. They will straggle uptown and catch up later.

Jesus says, "I'm hungry."

We settle into a diner on Ninth Avenue a couple of blocks from the seminary. Within a few minutes, the others join us. We look like we have been up for days. Outside, on the sidewalk, a man explodes in anger and dumps over a trash container, then stomps off cursing. Our rector goes out to tidy up.

"What's she doing?"

"Being pastoral to the trash can."

An hour later we are gathered in front of the chapel at the seminary, along with about twenty others, including a few who have come to gawk. We begin with some movement exercises to wake up—a mock tug-of-war and some graceful, stylized dancing with a length of rope. What begins as benign changes quickly. Suddenly, I am in the middle of a circle the crowd has formed. They grip the length of rope to mark my prison boundaries. We know that I have now become Jesus, even though the Jesus on trial is inside the chapel waiting for his big scene with Pilate.

The people in the circle, my jailers, are all friends, members of the parish, but they now hold this power over me. When I attempt to escape, they close ranks and tighten the rope against me. They are not laughing. Some of them glare at me fiercely, shout epithets, wag their heads. I rush them. They push back roughly, and I start to fall. One part of the line breaks to catch me. Pulling away, I sit on a curb while they stand around me, seemingly relaxed. They still hold the rope. We wait.

"So what are you going to do now, Jesus? Come on, you can get out! Try us. You're the Son of God, and all we've got is this rope!"

I do not move. It's a stand-off. If I do nothing, if I refuse to resist, then what?

Suddenly, it is the '60s, I am being dragged from my bed in the middle of the night. I am a student, a civil rights activist in Lynchburg, Virginia. And I think, as I lie curled in a ball on the floor, that these men are members of the American Nazi Party and kill people.

Pilate, wearing a black overcoat, steps out on the steps of the chapel. The official Jesus stands behind him and looks at me quizzically. Following the script, Pilate speaks to us about the need for order in society. Without warning, the crowd, now a mob that has abandoned the plan for the morning, rushes the steps and takes Jesus away, parading him around the close of the seminary, chanting abuse.

I am set free.

. . . . . .

38

MY PAGER GOES OFF at three o'clock one Sunday morning, catapulting me out of bed. As the weekend chaplain on call at St. Luke's Hospital, I have never been paged this late before. I think that there must be a serious emergency, someone in need of spiritual help, an accident victim, the distraught family of a dead child.

I call the number and hear that, once again, I am being paged to visit the dead. "We have a C.B. on nine," the nurse tells me. C.B. means: ceased breathing. No family is present, just the corpse.

"All right," I reply. "I'll be there in about thirty minutes. OK?"

My apartment is twenty blocks—a New York mile—from the hospital. The night is mild, the streets busier than they are in some places at noon. On Broadway, I flag a taxi and in the back seat put on my clerical collar. I carry a small bag containing a Prayer Book, Bible, consecrated host, identification badge, a small stole purple on one side and white on the other.

The sleepy guard at the desk waves me through without checking my I.D. The collar is all he needs to see. On the ninth floor, the nurse smiles quickly and points down the hall. "Twenty-three. Name's Rodriguez. I haven't wrapped him yet."

Most of the patients on nine have cancer. I know some of them from previous visits, but Rodriguez is new to me. He lies on his back, head turned slightly to the side, mouth open, eyes blank. An old man, bald, unshaven, nearly toothless. His body is scarcely visible under the sheets. I look at him carefully, taking in his features, as if I might see him tomorrow after church at the coffee hour. Ah, Mr. Rodriguez, how are you feeling today? He smiles, You remember me.

I remember you.

My friends look at me in amazement when I tell them that I visit the dead. They want to know what the point is. What kind of ministry can you perform for someone who is already dead? You do this in the middle of the night? They give me that "wacko" look.

I think about the women who go to the tomb where Jesus is buried. In Mark, Mary of Magdala, the mother of James, and Salome take aromatic oils to anoint the body. Luke omits Salome. In John, Mary of Magdala goes alone to mourn. Matthew says only that the two Marys come to "look at the grave." They go to see the body, to honor the dead, to mourn this man. The Early Church apparently made regular pilgrimages to visit the empty tomb as these early witnesses did. This is where they laid him, but there is no body. He is risen. The necessary connection between this life and the next, in Christian belief, is nonetheless through this body, and therefore through the tomb. Jesus is embodied, as are you and I. He dies, and so do we. And so we need to affirm the mortal body, as God does in the Incarnation, to know the Risen One.

I suspect that we prefer the risen Christ to the Jesus who suffers and dies because we look forward to that time when we will no longer suffer, when the identity at the root of our suffering is changed in God's love. The Christ affirms for us the continuity between life and death. They are one. Our embodied time is a small part of all that is, but it is the part that opens a window on the whole. Through Christ, and in us, the universe becomes enlightened.

But we cannot avoid the suffering, just as we cannot go around death. That is the other message of the Passion. The long liturgical preparation for the resurrection event reminds us that we have to go through all of it. There are no shortcuts, not even for Jesus.

Whenever the pager summons me to visit another one of us who has ceased to breathe, I go to honor the body and proclaim the resurrection. Often, I am the only one who can. The nurses call me when there are no relatives in town, when the one who has died is indigent, so that the dead will not go unremarked into darkness. Praying over the one who dies is also a tradition at St. Luke's Hospital. The nurses who call me are grateful when I come. My prayers at the body are for them closure, a way of saying goodbye to those they have cared for.

Mr. Rodriguez died alone. He had no family. He was one of those we pass every day on the street who smells of alcohol, tobacco, and feces. I imagine that I have smelled him before, one of those I look through on my way to someplace else.

Jesus tells us that he is among us as one of these outcasts, as a homeless man or woman on the street who begs us for food, water, shelter, clothing. Some say that he will not reveal himself to us again until we take seriously the command to feed and clothe the least among us.

I visit the dead as the Marys went to anoint Jesus. Mr. Rodriguez is Jesus dead, and if I don't go to visit him, there may be no resurrection. Jesus dies alone, but he rises among us. That seems to me a fundamental fact of Easter. Suppose no one goes to his tomb? Suppose the women who follow him go on down the road kicking dust and lamenting the end of the dream? Most of the disciples do run off when Jesus is crucified. They deny him. They give up. They allow fear to drive out their hopes.

But these women go back to honor the one who has lived among them. They want to remember. They do not go to the tomb to see a risen Lord. They go only to look, to anoint the body if they can, to affirm that this one has lived as they live.

They go to look on the one who has been pierced. And they see him as he is.

. . . . . .

39

DON HAS LEFT his wife and for the last four days has been on a drug binge in his old Harlem neighborhood. An hour ago he walked into the emergency room asking for a chaplain. The security guard called me at home. I have a cold. I am suspicious. I think Don wants money. But I go anyway.

"I don't need money," he says to me. "I need to talk to someone from the church. I want to go home."

"To your wife? Where is she now?"

He says he doesn't know but that his pastor might be able to find her. I offer to pay for a call to his pastor, who is three hours away in upstate New York. Don gets on the phone and rehearses his grievances against his wife. He wants someone to come to Manhattan and pick him up. The pastor says he will try to call Don's wife. I ask Don to let me talk to his pastor, who tells me that Don's mother and sister live in Manhattan and that Don has been visiting them regularly for the past six months.

I try to call his wife at home. There is no answer.

We go down the street to the Hungarian Pastry Shop to talk. It is eleven o'clock on a Saturday night. We are surrounded by Columbia University students deep in conversation.

Don has trouble staying awake. He says he has not slept in two days. I assume he is on something. He sips a coffee heavy with sugar, devours an apple tart.

"I lost it, you know? I was doing OK, in the Church, walking the way of Jesus, but then things happened. Like my wife. She starts accusing me of things. I bring home a friend who needs a hand and he's staying with us. She gets mad about it. Calls me a fag."

"She thinks you're gay?" Don nods off. "Hey! Wake up."

· · · · · ·

"Yeah. This is good coffee. I love coffee."

"Let's talk about what you're going to do. No one's coming to get you. You don't have money. How did you get here?"

"Car. It's out of gas. What I need right now is to get back my spirit. My spiritual life. That's what I need."

"I'm worried you'll go back to your drug friends."

He is nodding again. I urge him to his feet. We go out to the street.

"What I'd really like is one of those fifty-cent hot dogs."

I know what he means. There is a corner spot—it's called Papaya Something—a block away on Broadway. He continues to complain about his wife as we walk. At one point, he mentions his mother.

"Where is she?" I ask.

"Here in New York."

"Why don't you call her."

"That's not what I need. I need to get my spirit back. That's why I'm talking to you. Times like this, what you need is someone who will be with you."

Don gets two hot dogs with sauerkraut and relish. He has another coffee. We stand at a counter by the window and watch the street. He tells me about drug life in Harlem, hints he might have killed someone once. He chews and nods. I poke him regularly to keep him eating. It is almost one in the morning. I am tired. The security guard has told me Don can sit in the ER waiting room all night if he wants to. I tell him that and suggest we head back.

We walk up 110th Street, which is as busy now as it is at midday.

"Thing is this," Don says, "you got to be out where the people are to do the work of God, you know what I'm saying? That's the way it's supposed to be. The Gospel's got to be on its feet."

· · · · · ·

40

Aspergillum in hand and vested for Mass in full drag, I am blessing animals, mostly dogs, on West Forty-sixth Street. It is St. Francis's Day—actually the Sunday before the day—and I am feeling the Spirit. Some of the dogs are brought for blessings by those who know what today is. Others are simply out for the morning walk and encounter, happily, this grace. It is rare for someone to refuse a blessing for an animal. But it happens.

"Would your dog like a blessing?" I ask a man in a hurry. His dog, who might be a Lab, puts on the brakes. He wants a blessing. I can see it in his eyes. But the man on the other end of the leash drags him on.

I bless the animals by asperging them—sprinkling holy water—and this poor Lab gets a quick splash as he is yanked away. Bless you, I whisper.

Two big dogs get excited. One barks. The other leaps against me, almost knocking me over. The bowl of water in my hand slops over onto the dog's face. I sprinkle them both. "Bless you in the name of the Father, and the Son, and the Holy Spirit, and may the peace of St. Francis be with you always."

Woof.

One of the big dogs lunges against his leash, which momentarily chokes off his air. He falls in a lump, completely still. We all stare in shock. Have I blessed him to death?

"Happens all the time," says the man who loosens the adjustable collar. The dog leaps up and begins drinking holy water. I snatch it away. The man returns half an hour later with two more dogs of the same big size. He breeds them. I cast my blessing from a distance.

The cats, of course, blink, shrink, hiss. A parishioner shows up with a couple of seriously large cats who seem hardly to notice when I sprinkle them. Several people stop to ask if

I can bless their animals in absentia. Sure. I splash them with holy water and bless Muffy, and Hound, and Spot, and Cassius, and Gurrl. At least one dog needs a blessing because of bad behavior. Several are presented as being, themselves, blessings. But these are all good dogs and cats.

An actor shows up wearing an elephant nose, in honor of the parish production of *The Elephant Man*. (St. Clement's is also an off-Broadway theater.) He kneels in a most unelephant-like manner but looks sincere. I bless him (and all actors).

Each of the blessed receives a handwritten and illuminated "Certificate of Blessing." More than one person leaves money, and, by the end of the blessings—seventy-plus creatures later—the vet clinic we run for the pets of the homeless is $150 richer.

I like it, being on the street in my finery with a license to sprinkle and bless. Other clergy in the parish take their turns at blessing: the rector, Mother Crafton, does the early morning, Deacon Brooke the post-Eucharist, blessings. I imagine they like it as much as I do. Being out there with the animals is a Eucharist, thanksgiving for the creation. It is the sort of thing Francis would do every day—take the Church out into the street, bless the world as it is.

41

. . . . . .

IT IS ONE IN THE MORNING. There are twenty relatives in the hospital lobby, two of them weeping uncontrollably, one—sister of the dead man—screaming, "No, not again. No, I can't stand it." I go to her first, put my arms around her, pull her head to my chest. Her tears and saliva wet my shirt.

When her sobs subside, she tells me to go to the dead man's mother, who is standing rigidly in the center of the room. I put my hands on her shoulders. "I know he's with Jesus," she says, "but I don't know why."

I don't know why either. We only know that Anthony has been shot. Most of the adult male relatives drift outside to smoke, leaving the women to weep. The security guard who called me says I can take a small group up to see the body, which is still in the operating room. Ten of us crowd into the elevator. Anthony's mother and sister stay behind. A cousin carries Anthony's son, who is perhaps three years old.

It is one of those moments when I wonder what I am doing in this place with these people. They do not know me. All that we have in common is this dead man, a stranger to me. They are African-American. I am white. Somehow I am expected to comfort them and calm the situation. The guard has told me that he needs someone to bring the level of hysteria down. That is why he paged me at home. He looks uneasy, perhaps wondering if I can do it.

All of us go into the operating area in silence, with fear and trembling. Three nurses sit near by. They glance at us, then look away. I stand by Anthony's head. There is cotton over his eyeballs, giving him an other-worldly, almost alien look. His skin is a nutty brown, polished. Head shaved. A handsome man. The cousin holds Anthony's child in front of the dead face.

. . . . . .

"Say goodbye to your daddy," the cousin says. I cannot imagine how the boy will remember this scene.

I put my hand on the cold head.

It is the eighth time in the past week I have been in the hospital to give last rites to the dying or say prayers for the dead with relatives gathered, like this, around a bed. One widow asked me not to be too pious. A grandson picked up the Bible his sister had put on his grandmother's body and asked me, "I've never read this. Where do I start?" I told him, "Read the psalms. Start there."

All of these others pass through my mind as I read the prayer:

> Into your hands, O merciful Savior, we commend your servant
> Anthony. Acknowledge, we humbly beseech you, a sheep of your own
> fold, a lamb of your own flock, a sinner of your own redeeming.
> Receive him into the arms of your mercy, into the blessed rest of ever-
> lasting peace, and into the glorious company of the saints in light.

Together we say the Lord's Prayer. Two teenaged boys linger at the foot of the gurney as we begin to leave. They try to look at nothing. I touch one of them on the shoulder. He shrinks from me. The other's eyes fix on mine. There is a moment's silent intelligence between us.

I can almost hear the questions. Is Anthony with Jesus? What good does it do him or any of us for Anthony to be anywhere but right here where we need him? And who are those saints in light? Where can I go and look them in the face and demand they give him back to us?

Downstairs in the lobby, Anthony's sister is still weeping. His mother's eyes are dead. Everyone leaves quickly. We have nothing more to say to each other.

At 2:30 in the morning I am sitting in my apartment in the dark.

. . . . . .

42
· · · · · ·

BECAUSE HE IS A recovering alcoholic, a friend of mine does not take wine during Communion. Our theology of the Eucharist is that Christ is fully present in the ritual and in the elements and that in consuming either bread or wine, as our priest says, "you get everything." My friend still feels that he is missing something or that in declining the wine he is setting himself outside the community at its spiritual center. His sense of exclusion, of course, is more important to him and to me right now than the theology. We are sitting together in my parish office talking about how he might regain the sense of Christ's presence—but more importantly, of Christ's acceptance of him as he is.

That is the real issue for him. It raises for me other questions about what goes on in the Eucharist.

Another parishioner asks me one day, "Do we believe that the bread and wine actually become the body and blood of Christ?"

We—that is, Episcopalians—believe that Christ is truly present in the consecrated elements, which is not the same as saying that they materially *become* Christ's body and blood. The presence we acknowledge is spiritual but not, for that, any less real. Bread and wine not consumed during the Eucharist are reserved in a tabernacle on or near the altar. A burning candle or light informs us that Christ is present. I suspect that it is difficult for most people to understand how this mystery works. My guess is that our thinking is closer to magic than it is to sacrament.

Magical thinking says that the celebrant waves her hands over the bread and wine, says the magic words, and *voila!*: Christ is really present. One priest said to a parishioner who

· · · · · ·

asked what would happen if a layman celebrated the Eucharist, It would be like saying grace before lunch."

Which means, nothing happens.

For me the Eucharist is a community ritual in which the priest, the person authorized to preside, acts on our behalf to bring us into God's presence. The consecration of the bread and wine is a consecration of the community as one set apart in the Spirit. Christ is truly present among us, and the bread and wine represent that presence. The bread and wine on the altar are a continuous reminder that we are one in the Spirit because we share one meal. No magic occurs, but the priest consecrates because we have ordained—selected—her to be the one who represents our ritual life in this way.

My friend's understanding of what happens in the Eucharist is based on the notion that the bread and the wine in themselves are sacred objects once they are consecrated. They are sacred, and remain sacred, in the context of community. But when an inquisitive parishioner asks, "If I give someone consecrated bread, but he doesn't know it's consecrated, has he consumed the body of Christ?" my answer is that he has not. What happens in Eucharist is a community event. Christ is not for me alone. The community accepts my friend as he is, because he is part of us, and in taking bread we give him all that we have. We are as fully present as Christ in Communion. My friend's issue is that he does not believe that we love him.

And so his issue is our issue too.

. . . . . .

43

A THIRD EYE in the forehead. It is what I think when I see people in the streets on Ash Wednesday. All of them have been given this eye in the head by someone who has a bizarre sense of humor. I cannot get over their wanting this ominous smudge. I have often thought that the mark of Cain was a third eye that never closed.

After eating pancakes on Shrove Tuesday, we fill a galvanized tin bucket with ratty old palms from last year and toss in a match. They whoosh into flame like woods in a drought. We step back. Our priest invites all of us to toss in a palm fragment and, with it, a piece of our lives that we wish to change or be rid of. Burn up a part of yourself for Lent. I choose something I've thrown away before; it keeps returning. We will use the ashes of our lives tomorrow on Ash Wednesday.

We forget to open the windows and doors first. The room fills with smoke. It is like a circle of hell for a while, shadowy figures lurching and coughing in the haze while a fire flickers on the walls.

The next day I go with two parishioners to the hospital to impose ashes on patients and staff. We tour the wards, beginning with the emergency room. Eagerly, nurses and orderlies line up. Because there are several of us, we move into the "trauma room," which a nurse tells me is not used that often. I say it is a good place for this liturgy.

I rub my thumb into the oily ashes while one of my friends reads the collect for the day and then, as I make the sign of the cross on each forehead, the other parishioner reads from Psalm 51:

> Have mercy on me, O God, according to your loving-kindness;
> In your great compassion blot out my offenses.

And as I mark them I whisper, "Remember that you are dust and to dust you shall return." During the afternoon I give thirty-five people this news that each desires to hear. I solemnly condemn each one of them to death, and every one looks at me as if I had said "you will live forever."

One Ash Wednesday in the intensive care ward I watched doctors and nurses frantically try to save a man's life, opening his chest, massaging his heart, not an hour after I had put ashes on his head and told him the truth he then entered. After he died, the nurses who had failed to save him lined up for their ashes outside the room where his body lay.

Who would have thought there was such hunger for mortality? I think that we have a need to see it, our end, even as we wish to deny it in ourselves and in others. Liturgy is good for us in just this way. It allows us to look at the things we want to avoid. It invites us into a safe space where reality, like an eye, can be opened, where truth can be touched and eaten. The Eucharist is like that, except that no one else can see that we are walking around the streets with God in our bellies. Nor can anyone see that years ago, before we knew anything, a priest marked our foreheads with holy oil, following Baptism, and declared that we are "Christ's own forever."

And touching the exact same place—I think about it as I press my thumb into another forehead, brushing aside a lock of hair—I commend these bodies to the earth from which they came. I open the eye with which they can see themselves, like blind Bartimaeus who gets up when he has been healed and follows Jesus on the way to the cross.

· · · · · ·

44

· · · · · ·

THE OTHER DEACON in my parish calls at eleven o'clock on Friday night. She tells me that our rector has been attacked by a drunk during the intermission of a play in which she is performing at the church. He pushed her down, probably twice, when she tried to stop him as he stormed up the stairs to the theater. Who knows why; he was drunk. A member of the cast overpowered him.

When an ambulance took her to a local hospital, the police took him to the precinct station. I am not far from the hospital. I get dressed and flag a taxi. Although there is nothing for me to do there, and I know that others are with her and that the injuries are not serious (she is bruised and has a gash on her arm), I go because it is what I do as an ordained person. My ordination does not give me a choice. I am under a vow of obligation to and by and for the Church.

A Roman Catholic priest I know was attacked in the rectory by a deranged, homeless man one morning. It was quick. His attacker rang the rectory bell and, when the priest opened the door, slashed him with a knife. I came by half an hour later on an errand and discovered the young parish secretary in tears. A police officer was still there, but he was no help to her. The priest had been taken to the hospital. The phone was ringing. I picked it up because the secretary was in shock, and I spent the next hour answering phones as parishioners called in to find out what had happened. My job was simply to be reassuring until the priest was released from the hospital. Word of the attack spread with unbelievable speed. He was not seriously hurt, but he was shaken by the experience. We all were. It reminded those of us doing regular pastoral care in the city that we are always at risk.

These are small events—answering the phone, going to the hospital. That is where the

· · · · · ·

ministry takes place, in these small corners. When we hosted the annual Broadway Blessing at the parish (an interfaith service for the performers and directors of the season's new plays), I vested with the visiting clergy from the Lutheran and Roman Catholic Churches even though I had no official role to play. I simply sat there. Later, our rector said that she was sorry I did not have anything to do. I replied that I am to be present. That is my contribution. My vocation is to bear witness.

And so I get out of bed on this Friday night to be present for my rector and parish. As the taxi speeds down the West Side Highway, I think about that obligation to be there when called. It comes up often in my life, not only in the Church. Because I am one who wants to be noticed, who wants to be at the center of attention, it is hard for me simply to be present, do nothing, be part of the furniture. I have to work at it.

By the time I get to the hospital, our priest has already been discharged. I walk over to the church, a few blocks away, and two other parishioners are there. But she has already gone home. We hang around and talk for a while. There is nothing to do. I trudge back to the subway, trailed by a parishioner who wants to talk about some personal problems. We stand on the corner for several minutes, but I want to go. My own needs suddenly intrude. I cannot hear what the man in front of me is saying, but I wait until there is a pause into which I insert a perfunctory, "God bless," and dash down the stairs to catch the subway.

One part of the evening haunts me. When the taxi drops me at the hospital, the driver asks if anything serious has happened. When I tell him that the priest in our parish has been injured, he asks if he should come in and give blood. It is an astonishing offer from a man whose living depends on his keeping in motion. The more he drives, the more he can make. We have not spoken at all during the trip downtown. He looks Pakistani, probably not a Christian. He makes this simple offer, and I believe he will give blood if I accept.

He is not obligated to me or the Church to do anything.

45
. . . . . .

THE SISTERS of the Community of the Holy Spirit in Brewster, New York, have filled in their swimming pool and covered it with a version of the labyrinth so popular in spiritual practice these days. Situated on a small rise overlooking the Melrose School and St. Cuthbert's Retreat House, both run by the order—and next to a playground and parking lot—the location does not at first promise meditative silence. Arriving early for a parish retreat, I take the opportunity to walk the labyrinth, even though I am suspicious of the practice. Although the form itself is ancient—a medieval example can be found on the floor of Chartres Cathedral—walking the thing still suggests to me a New Age sacrament, conferring an easy grace.

A labyrinth is not like a maze, which is designed to mislead. There are no high walls or boxwood hedges, no dead ends. Whereas a maze is supposed to get you lost, a labyrinth is intended to show the way. Only a third of a mile long, it is a path, marked by lines on the floor or pavement, that folds in multiple turns and switchbacks around a central point. There is one way in and one way out. Seen from above, the labyrinth is pleasing geometry, abstractly beautiful.

The early afternoon sun bears unbroken on the concrete path. Since the recommended time to walk is early morning or evening, I count on being alone in the June heat. Because school is out, I count on silence. I begin to sweat. My plan is to walk this labyrinth as slowly as possible. Understanding that I am entering holy ground, I take off my shoes.

As in Zen meditation, I empty my mind and focus on the repeated act of walking. My steps are small, measured. I am not going anywhere, not to Jerusalem—which was the metaphorical destination of the earliest designs—nor even to the center of the labyrinth

. . . . . .

itself. The end of this journey belongs to the one who walks it. The pilgrimage itself is the point, as all prayer is its own end.

I have to resist the impulse to speed up, to walk faster, so that I can get back to the retreat house and join the others who are gathering on the porch to drink iced tea. For someone from New York City, this purposeless walk is painful. Every cell in my body is screaming: Hurry! We have to get there now! This is the same impulse that makes me leave for an airport thirty minutes sooner than I know I have to. This meditative walk is for one as restless as I am a necessary discipline: I need to learn to *be*.

At the center of the labyrinth is a small concrete block, not even a foot high. Once I reach it, I sit on it in a half-lotus for fifteen minutes, looking back over the tortuous path I have traveled. At first the center has a calming influence on me, but then I feel that I am looking back at my own sometimes convoluted life and, leaping up, begin to speed walk the return path. There is a moment's panic. Then I force myself to slow down until I am barely moving. The sweat begins to run down my back and into my eyes. I watch my shuffling feet so that I will not be looking toward the cool grass at the end of the journey.

After another hour of excruciatingly slow movement, I emerge from the labyrinth drenched and drained. Feeling as if I have been in a desert, where there is no other life but that of the Spirit, I make my way quickly to the porch of the retreat house. I need to be among other bodies. Jesus must have felt that same need after his time in the labyrinth of his own desert. For him, of course, Jerusalem and the death it represented were at the center of his pilgrimage. For me it is not that clear. I know that I glimpsed one of my own demons and tried to run away from it.

I have been nowhere and accomplished nothing. During my walk in the labyrinth, I said no prayers. My mind was empty. I thought about nothing. I walked in the hot sun for two hours (probably four times as long as the average time spent in a labyrinth). I imagine that pilgrimage is exactly like this—long and boring, often hot, lacking logical purpose. In Islam it is an obligation to go to Mecca once in a lifetime. But the life of the Spirit is not about space. God is not about place. Even a pilgrimage to Mecca is not about going to Mecca.

And Jerusalem is never just Jerusalem.

I realize, back on the porch sipping iced tea, that the beauty of the labyrinth is the way it transforms space into time, making pilgrimage a journey of the Spirit instead of a trip from one place to another. In the labyrinth, I am not only going nowhere, I am in no place. Every labyrinth is the same—the one at Grace Cathedral in San Francisco, at Chartres, here in Brewster. Inside the labyrinth, there is no location, only the presence of God. And the walk is our practice of that presence for our own lives.

46

DOUG, A DOORMAN in my apartment building, gives me a concerned look as I pass through the lobby. He knows that when I am wearing my clerical collar someone has probably died. But it is Sunday, and I tell him I am on my way to the church.

He smiles. "OK, reverend. You preaching?"

When I say that I am, he holds me briefly by my elbow. "You should tell people about what's happening. You know, how those Nostradamus predictions are coming true."

"They are?" Although I am late, I want to hear more.

"Well, you can begin to see the signs. There was that tornado in Utah. When was the last time there was a tornado there? Never, that's when. An earthquake in Las Vegas—6.5 on the Richter scale. Pretty unusual, I'd say. Then yesterday there was a flood on the Long Island Expressway. Five inches of rain on the road. And of course the eclipse."

Right. The eclipse. I had not thought that anyone regarded it as a sign of the world's end, but given the proximity to the new millennium others were concerned. Later, I saw a headline in *El Diario*, the Manhattan Spanish-language newspaper I read to keep up my Spanish: "Eclipse no es el fin del mundo: Walter Mercado." (Mercado is an astrologer.) The article says that the Church's position is clear: no one knows the date the world will end; the eclipse is a natural phenomenon.

Doug, however, remains concerned. His coworker on the desk agrees. "The signs are everywhere," he says gravely.

I have not read Nostradamus. Does he make predictions about Las Vegas and the Long Island Expressway? The drought this year has been bad. My mother tells me that a perfectly healthy tree in their backyard has fallen over during the night: there is not enough moisture to keep the root system in place. I have never heard of a tree falling down on its own. Perhaps it happens all the time. I do not mention this to Doug, fearing to add to his concerns.

After I leave the building, I wonder if Doug really believes what he has been saying. Does he fear the end of the world? Worse yet, do he and those who are fascinated by predictions of the end actually desire it? I would prefer that the world continue. My life is better than it has been in years. I can honestly say that I am happy. My children are in college. I want to see them grow into the people they have begun to be. Finally, I have come to know my parents as human beings. I enjoy being with them. For the first time in my adult life I am free of the anxieties that have plagued me. This would be a bad time to end the world. (As a man in my parish is fond of saying, "It's all about me, of course.")

What is it like, I wonder, to put your faith in Nostradamus or in Walter Mercado and her (yes, *her*) astrological predictions? What is it like to live in fear that God intends to end everything *just because it's time*? What is it like to live that way?

I want to tell him that God is not a terrorist planning to wipe us out. The millennium is only a click on the odometer. Our fears have given it a meaning that time itself does not have, because time is completely neutral and artificial. We made it up.

Here is the message for every year of our lives, Doug: God still dwells among us. We have nothing to fear.

. . . . . .

47

IT IS A FRIGID MORNING, the first work day of the year 2000, and I head reluctantly to the office. All night the wind has rapped on the windows of my apartment twenty-seven floors above Broadway. The windows slide sideways to open, and I usually leave a space for fresh air, even in winter. I do the morning's Zen meditation under the window, through which today's frigid air pours. I imagine that I am a Buddhist monk sitting in the cold of a Japanese temple. (This is the romanticizing of one's life that Zen is supposed to cure.)

Passing through the lobby on my way out, I overhear someone say, "Well, that's the way it is. You're born, you die, you go to heaven or hell. That's it."

I have heard similar sentiments before. "Life's a bitch. Nobody gets out alive." The implication seems to be: What's the point in doing anything? Where does it go? Who cares?

On the train to my office I have been reading a book, *From the Zen Kitchen to Enlightenment*, based on the work of a twelfth-century Zen master named Dogen, which says that the work of the *tenzo*, the one who prepares meals in the monastery, is the highest form of devotion. It is like doing meditation. Those who prepare food with the same attention they bring to prayer or worship understand the nature of things. The servers of food know the difference between washing sand and washing rice.

Dogen writes: "My personal life experience is at the same time the world of reality." In other words, that empty stretch of time between birth and death is the place in which we know the world as it is. Birth and death are not meaningful experiences for us. And whether one goes to heaven or hell is not our business. All that matters is cooking the rice.

When I am riding the train from Manhattan to New Rochelle, all that matters is riding the train. This time is not meaningless. It is not just about getting from one place to another. This morning I am not paying attention and go to the track on which I normally catch the train, but it is not there. Another train is on track 24. When I walk into the car, I realize that there is something wrong, even though the train looks just like mine. I cannot say why. I just know that it is not my train. It is not my life.

Sometimes I meditate on the train; usually I read, but not to "pass the time." Dogen's essay on being the cook ("How to Cook Your Life") reminds us that everything we do can have meaning or purpose. To identify parts of my life as being of no consequence is to squander all of my life. I do not live in separated spheres, some of which are purer or more purposeful than others.

We see this holistic attitude toward existence in the life of Jesus as well. For him a meal with friends is significant. It is good to eat and drink. He takes time. And that, I think, is the point: that we "take time" in our lives, rather than allowing time to take us, as if we were a leaf or cork dropped into a stream to be carried to whatever end awaits. Taking time, however, is not the same thing as making something happen. Jesus does not make something happen. He is what happens. When I understand my life as being identical with reality, I am also what happens.

48

IT IS THE FIRST SUNDAY after the Epiphany, and I enter the sacristy wearing an Egyptian *gallabya*—the tunic-like garment men wear in parts of the Middle East. It is one of my favorite things. I feel safe in it, although I do not know why that should be. Lately, I have been wearing it to sleep. In the sacristy, one of the servers guesses that might be so. "Jammies?" she inquires.

I put a dalmatic over the jammies, my stole over dalmatic, and join the procession. Today is the "one-rehearsal pageant" at St. Clement's, a twenty-five-year tradition in which dogs might appear as sheep, the angels wear top hats, and the Star of Bethlehem steals the show by cavorting through the congregation as it leads the kings (or queens) to the manger. This year the baby Jesus is a stuffed animal, Eyore from *Winnie the Pooh*. It had been suggested that we use a dog, but that was too much even for St. Clement's, a notoriously dog-friendly parish.

My job is to be the head shepherd. Three children wearing pillow cases knotted at the corners to make ears learn in the one rehearsal to follow me. That is all they need to know. I carry a stuffed sheep under my arm as a sign of my vocation.

The pageant is a hit, as always—funny and yet, at the same time, moving. It is effective in ways other pageants are not, because it does not take itself too seriously. There is a kind of "we're just bozos on this bus" quality to the event that is touching. The sheep-children are excited about the baby Jesus but also amused because they know what is really in the blanket. One of the parish actors has dressed as a donkey, complete with baseball-cap ears, but he looks more like a rabbit.

This is good church—fun, inventive, somewhat chaotic. But then there is a problem.

Someone has scheduled a lunch for the parish hall but neglected to tell the organizers of the coffee hour who came early to set up. In the kitchen, ham is cooking, part of a traditional after-church lunch on this Sunday. Several people are upset about the miscommunication. One expresses his anger to the cook, who later tells me that he only does what he's told. There are hurt feelings. Who allowed this to happen? Why can't this church be a "real" church that plans and executes effectively?

Those who are upset are right, of course. People should talk to each other. They should be considerate, aware of what is going on. This church is small. It should be easy to coordinate these things. But on the other hand, the church is more than an institution. It is ironic that on the Sunday of the one-rehearsal pageant, which is an emblem of spontaneity, there should be a struggle over scheduling. Does it matter if there is a coffee hour and a lunch at the same time? Not really. People can do both. Those who want only coffee will have coffee and go home.

The lesson of the pageant, and indeed one of the lessons of the circumstances of the birth of Jesus, is that life unfolds as it should and as it can. We may want to control it. We may wish it were more organized. We may wish that there were room at the inn or a friendlier political atmosphere. But our lives are not institutions. The pageants of our lives are performed without rehearsal.

And sometimes in our jammies.

49

I AM ONE OF THE PEOPLE who helps set up the room for weekly sittings at Still Mind Zendo (a zendo is a place where one does Zen meditation). This one is located in a loft in a midtown Manhattan building that in ordinary time is used as an acting and dance studio. We unpack the wooden box containing the objects for the altar: a bowl for water, vase of dried flowers, incense holder, candle, a white statue of the seated Buddha. We arrange the mats in two parallel rows, set the screens in front of the mirrors along one wall, place the gong and timer, incense and matches where they belong. I then stand inside the door to the room and greet, by bowing with hands together in front of my chin, those entering the space. This bow of greeting is called *gassho*. We bow to our mat, the person we meet, and the Buddha.

We do not pray to the Buddha. Those of us who are Christians or Jews are careful about that. Our bow to the statue, like our bows to each other, are signs of respect. The Buddha represents the dharma, the universal teachings embodied by the Buddha, Jesus, Moses, and Mohammed. My prayer in that space every week is one of listening for the dharma.

In the time I have been sitting Zen, I have learned how to listen in prayer. That has been the great gift of this tradition. Sitting in silence and allowing myself to be part of the emptiness of all things, I have learned to give up illusions of control—the illusions that I can manage a conversation with God, that I can control the emptiness with my desires, that I can live apart from all that is. When we give up our illusions of control, what is left is awareness.

Zen koans are doors to awareness. They seem to be puzzles, or intellectual games, but in fact they resist efforts to be understood intellectually. They reveal themselves in meditation, often with explosive clarity. One of the most important koans is this one: "A monk once asked Joshu, 'Does a dog have the Buddha Nature?' Joshu answered, '*Mu!*'"

The word "*mu*" has a negative connotation—it more or less means "not." (As is often the case in Zen, meaning is intentionally elusive.) For a while, I was sitting with this koan, walking around thinking about it during the day. I did not know what it meant or how to explain it, but it is a door to prayer, in the same way scripture can be a door to prayer. (I have also been sitting with the sayings of Jesus in the Gospel of Thomas.) The *mu* koan is about listening, I think, and one morning, while I was sitting in my apartment focused on it, I suddenly heard this: "Be exactly who you are but do not want it." It was as if someone had spoken aloud.

I immediately put my hands together in front of my chin and bowed. Although not an answer to prayer—for example, please tell me what *mu* means—this experience was a demonstration of prayer as listening.

Not too long after, I participated in my first all-day sitting at the zendo. I was not sure what to expect. We were to sit, with breaks for tea and lunch, from 9:30 to 5:30, trying to "stay in the room." The mind wants to wander away in search of problems, anxieties, other rooms. It is like sitting for two hours, only longer, I told myself. You can do this.

Greg, the head monk, asked if I would carry and light the incense for each of the day's sittings. He explained what was involved. I agreed. How hard could it be? Walking into the zendo to the right of Janet, our teacher, I realized that I was once more taking the role of a deacon. I bent over the candle on the altar and touched the incense stick to the flame. But I miscalculated. The stick extinguished the fire. I felt my face flush with embarrassment. Without looking at Janet, who stood passively nearby, I picked up the matchbook lying behind the Buddha and attempted to relight the candle. The first effort failed. I struck a second match, acutely aware of the silence this sound of striking matches violated.

I remembered the time I proudly proclaimed the wrong Gospel lesson one Sunday at St. Mary's, the first time I spilled wine down the front of a woman's white blouse, the day in the Cathedral when I forgot to pause for the bishop's blessing before reading the Gospel. One of the first things deacons learn about doing liturgy is to remain focused on the task at hand and forget about the mistakes. Dwelling on them only leads to others. This is also the lesson of Zen: stay in the moment.

The candle was finally lit. The incense was burning. I stepped back to my mat and began the day's sitting. Knowing that I would focus on my error, I decided to block it out by sitting with the *mu* koan for the morning. With each exhalation of breath, I formed in my mind the sound "*mu*." Obsessively, however, I returned to the moment when I snuffed the candle with the stick of incense. The battle was joined. I imagined what Janet must think of me. *MU*! Everyone in the zendo had to be amazed at my incompetence. *MU*! I saw myself stuck in the time of my revealed failings. Look at the man who does not know how to light incense properly! His hands are trembling. *MU*!

At the end of the first hour, I had a meeting with Janet for a dialogue known in Japanese as *daisan*, during which the student discusses the state of his practice with the teacher. After I explained my effort to combat my mistake with the *mu* koan, she said, "Be careful that *mu* does not just become another illusion. Everything is *mu*, including the snuffed candle."

Mu is not a tool. It is not to be used to fill up the mind with static in order to keep out distracting or negative thoughts. I have misused the Jesus prayer in this way as well: "Lord Jesus Christ, have mercy on me, a sinner." Repeating it when I am anxious or unable to sleep, I numb myself with the mantra. The point, however, is not to anesthetize. The point is to become aware, to awaken. Prayer should open eyes, not close them.

Back in the zendo, I breathed again with *mu* but not this time in opposition to the snuffing of the candle but with it. I put out the flame. *MU*! I relight the wick. *MU*! I breathe. *MU*!

The dog *is* Buddha nature.

. . . . . .

50

A MEMBER OF MY PARISH is leaving today for a six-week visit to India, where she will be continuing her training as a yoga instructor. Although she goes by her Western name in the parish, she is known as Padmashri at the yoga center where she works in Manhattan. Asking for Pamela there will get you no one. The two names are telling. She is a Christian, who feels called to ordained ministry, practicing yoga as a religious exercise. In India, she will be in an ashram participating in Hindu devotions.

Increasingly, people of faith will be like Padmashri. They will be like the people who sit together at the Still Mind Zendo. They will be like my friend Katherine, who is a pastor in a Presbyterian Church and a member of B'Nai Jeshurun Congregation on the Upper West Side of Manhattan. In my work as editor of an interreligious journal, I see articles every week about this question of religious identity, especially by Christians seeking to expand the boundaries of their once triumphalist faith. It is no longer possible to insist that all people must come to Christ to be saved. Nor, I think, is it possible to say that Christ works in all people of faith, whether they know it or not.

The work I do has helped convince me that religious boundaries are collapsing, at least as people actually practice religion. If anything, however, institutions are becoming more, even exclusively, concerned about clarifying their identities. Struggles over orthodoxy in my denomination, the Episcopal Church, have intensified. The Roman Catholic Church has become more rigid, Orthodox Judaism more demanding in Israel, Islam more exacting. The issue is controlling identity as a defense against the encroaching sands of pluralism.

But when I visit people in the hospital or talk with those who write for *Cross Currents*, I hear none of that rigidity, little of the concern for orthodoxy that consumes organizations.

The sick are usually happy to see me whatever their religious affiliations. Those who write for the journal are busily exploring the boundary waters. A recent contributor spoke convincingly about the dangers of monotheism. If there is any tenet of my faith I assumed to be unassailable, it is monotheism—and yet this article led me to question even that assumption. Another article in the journal suggests that we are entering a period of "Christianness," in which the institutions called Christianity dissolve, as Christendom's political and social order did in the nineteenth century, leaving us with a way of being that is characterized as Christ-inspired. The author speaks of a Christic consciousness, perhaps not unlike Krishna consciousness, that leaves the Church as institution behind.

I love this intellectual provocation. But I also experience Christianity as edifice, substantiality. It is as much about things as it is about the Spirit: chalices, cathedrals, food, books. Would "Christianness" be enough for a faith so rooted in the body? The resurrection is not about transcending body. It is about affirming body. The Body of Christ is celebration of the thingness of human life and belief. The institution bears witness. Some days I hate it.

The last Sunday before leaving, Padmashri says, "I wish you were coming with me." And for a moment, I break free of institutional chains and fly to India where Christic consciousness is perfect, as nothing can be.

51
. . . . . .

CHRIS, A PARISHIONER, calls me back only a few minutes after we have finished a one-hour telephone conversation. "Ken," she says, emotionally, "Barbara needs our prayers. Q has been carjacked and kidnapped."

Barbara is the priest in charge of St. Clement's Church. Q is the nickname for her husband, Richard. The words "carjacked" and "kidnapped" mean, in my experience, that someone is going to be found dead.

"What happened?"

"I don't know for sure. She took the train home. Q was meeting her in the parking lot at Metropark in New Jersey. They were jumped. She was pushed out of the car. She's at the police station. I'm going there now. We need to pray for Q."

I call some others in the parish. We are all shocked and helpless. I stand at the window of my apartment looking across the river to New Jersey, where Q is a hostage or dead. He is an older man, a professor, not someone accustomed to being under this kind of stress. I worry that he will have a heart attack. Looking at the Palisades, I try to project prayer. Lord, keep Q safe. God, don't let him die. Jesus, be with Barbara.

It seems futile. How many of us are offering prayers just like that? Unvarnished pleas for help. No Book of Common Prayer niceties here. Just elemental fear and need.

My friend Kathy is out of town. She calls while I am standing at the window. When I tell her what has happened, she says, urgently, "Call Carol!"

Carol is psychic. She prays for people. She prays constantly, in fact—and as one who has been the object of her prayers, I know that she manages, in some way, to project confidence in God's grace into apparently hopeless situations.

. . . . . .

I call her. "I'll get right on it," she says.

In general, I have trouble praying for something like the release of a hostage or the lifting of particular burdens. It is unseemly to bargain with God, and such prayers often seem like bartering. Here I am, Lord. I want your help, right now, for this exact need of mine. That is a long way from: Your will be done. Might it be God's will that Q die? I doubt that. I do not believe that God wills death in that way. But it is true that Q will die, as I will, and perhaps tonight is his night and this terrifying moment his death. If it is, then we are all part of his dying. We are united in his peril. In that alone, our prayer has had an effect. Around the city, and in New Jersey, we are connected deeply through our common faith that God acts with us for our good.

Carol calls me. "What kind of car do they have?" she wants to know. I am not sure. "It's OK. I've seen something. A blue foreign car. But it doesn't matter. I think it's all right." She returns to her prayers. A few minutes later, Chris calls me back.

"He's safe. He's at home. The guy made him drive to Newark and then let him go."

"What color is their car?"

"Huh?"

"Is it blue?"

"Time to go to bed, Ken."

I make some calls to others to tell them the good news. It is midnight. We have been at prayer for two hours. Carol is relieved but not surprised.

"You're good," I tell her.

All of us are good. Because we live our lives in prayer, because we know prayer as a normal occurrence, we bear witness to God's presence in such times. That is the answer to prayer—not the delivery of goods but the certainty of presence.

. . . . . .

52

I HAVE BEEN HAVING DREAMS about the Presiding Bishop of the Episcopal Church. They began when he was elected to this office as the head of the Church in the United States and moved to New York City. He was a spiritual mentor to me when I came back to the Church in the early '80s, but we have not seen each other in years.

In the first dreams, two or three of them over a couple of months, I feel a strong sense of longing. He does not appear in them, but I know that the person I want to see is the Presiding Bishop. This longing is mixed with annoyance that he is in the city and has not called me. The dreams are disturbing. Since I have just been ordained a deacon, I wonder if my dreams are about some sort of closure with this important figure in my spiritual growth. Deacons serve under their bishops, and I think for a while that I am looking for his ecclesiastical approval.

Then I have a funny dream in which I steal the Presiding Bishop's throne and hide it in the attic. Although the PB (as we refer to him) has a cathedra, a kind of throne, in the Washington National Cathedral, I do not have an attic. The place in which I put the throne is filled with costumes of various sorts, a kind of theatrical closet. Stealing the throne works. He shows up looking for it and is surprised to find that I am the one who has taken it. He is also amused—"Isn't this curious," he says—and the dream ends with his laughter.

The next dream is one in which I am with the PB at his apartment, which is a penthouse on top of the headquarters of the Episcopal Church in Manhattan. His wife is there. She and I have spoken on the telephone two or three times since their arrival in the city. In the dream, she tells me with some urgency that she cannot find someone to deliver *The New*

York Times by 6 A.M. when the PB wants to read it. He smiles benevolently at me, and I feel momentarily ashamed to be noticed by him at all.

The dreams stopped then for about three months, and I was glad that they were gone. They made me feel like an adolescent. I discussed them with my good friend Ken, and we surmised that they had something to do with my father, who is in poor health and with whom I have had a difficult relationship. The dreams might signify my yearning for his love and approval, certainly something that has been true in my life. And yet that sense of need had not been there in some time. It felt wrong. I was in another place with my father, one beyond longing and more like acceptance.

Perhaps, Ken suggested, I truly was annoyed that the PB was not my intimate, that since he had been in the city we had not had the private time together we once had. But I doubted that this was so. The dreams felt more substantial than that. They seemed to be about more than hurt feelings or a longing for a past relationship. The truth was, I did not want to go backward in my life. I was living exactly the life I am called to live—and there was no doubt that the PB was instrumental in my being who I am.

The last dream is a very simple one. The PB and I are walking together, perhaps at the Jesuit retreat center where we went on several occasions when I was at St. Martin's. We stop in a grove on the center's grounds. He puts an arm around my shoulder and says, simply, "You are my beloved son."

I woke up, startled, and said aloud the name of the one I had been seeking, the dream's true subject, the one who has called me: "God."

53

A POLITE AFRICAN-AMERICAN OFFICER asks me to put my hands behind my back. I comply. He tightens the plastic handcuffs around my wrists. "I wish I didn't have to do this," he says.

Along with seventy-five other Episcopalians, most of them ordained, I am being arrested for blocking the entrance to the headquarters of the New York City Police Department. Outside the building, five hundred demonstrators noisily support our arrest.

We are part of a series of demonstrations organized in New York City to protest official indifference to the killing of an unarmed West African immigrant named Amidou Diallo, whom the police shot in a fusillade of forty-one bullets. The killing is a sign of deteriorating relations between the government and communities of color in the city. More bluntly: black people are being stopped in huge numbers on the streets, and they are afraid. The rest of us are feeling that fear too.

We are taken in police vans to different precincts around the city for booking—twelve of us in each van. Few of us have been arrested before. There are jokes, uneasy hilarity. The police go out of their way to be courteous. It is nothing like arrests in the '60s, for example, when detention by the police was often brutal. All of us are on a list previously submitted to the police. We know that we will be given a summons for disorderly conduct and released, probably within six hours. We are detained in the precinct squad room, not in a jail cell, and have access to snack food and a free telephone. We are *allowed* to be here. Every now and then young black men in metal handcuffs and scruffy clothes are hustled through on the way to their cells. One of the officers refers to these as "real prisoners." We all, both blacks and whites, feel the sting of that.

"I'm a real prisoner," objects a priest in a double-breasted, pinstriped suit. It is what we want to be.

Near the time of our release, late in the afternoon, we hold a service of Evening Prayer. It is the Feast of the Annunciation. During the long afternoon, the point has become clear. None of us can leave until the police say we can. Even though we are not behind bars, there are still forty of us in a small, cramped space. The handcuffs have been removed, but most have been standing for hours. Muscles ache. Anxiety appears on several faces. The jokes become strained. The polite officers still look tough. They wear bullet-proof vests and carry guns. We are real prisoners.

Some of us are veterans of the social-justice movements of the '60s. It has been a long time since I left the protection of my comfortable life.

The life of the Spirit includes doing time, even this easy time. Jesus does time. He serves it among us, incarnate in flesh. He comes down from heaven, as we say in the creed, the ancient way of saying what we believe. And then he is set free. He ascends (disappears in a way not quite like death), leaving us to mill around down here in custody, wondering what happens next. We have little choice. We are here and cannot get out alive.

We call the season of Pentecost "ordinary time." After the extraordinary time in which Jesus lives among us—his birth, ministry, death, and resurrection—we are left with the common ticking of daily life. We do the time. We wait for Christ to come again, whatever that means.

But ordinary time is also holy time. Common things are also sacred objects. In the Eucharist, we use ordinary dishes and simple foods. We have been washed into Christ's death with plain water. We worship in the bodies in which we also work, make love, and play. We become the assembly of God through and in the common. There is no other way.

· · · · · ·

These are also the bodies that suffer injustice, here and in every place and time. As I write this, bombs are falling on Yugoslavia, where Serbian forces continue a genocidal assault on ethnic Albanians. Amidou Diallo is dead forever. There is a meanness in the greed of this new century that begins to feel threatening. We have bought safe streets and wealth at the expense of the poor and the nonwhite. A taxi I take from the airport is stopped at one of the increasingly common roadblocks in Manhattan. A rude officer demands my immigrant driver's papers and threatens to arrest him if he does not hurry. My black friends are regularly stopped and frisked for no reason.

Against such offenses our simple worship seems inadequate, our mild and carefully-managed protest silly. Do well-dressed, witty Episcopalians detained by the police for six hours bring the love of Christ into the world? It is a place to begin. All of life is equally common and equally sacred. That is not a formula for quietism. Privatized religion—religion that has no political face, which is practiced only in sacred time and space, in prayer or in ecstasy—is the temptation Christians always face. It is the deadly temptation to "be spiritual." What we do in the Church needs to be what we do every day. We have to do the time with others. Self-serving religiosity is not enough.

What our faith teaches us most profoundly is how to do the time with awareness. It is the way Jesus lives, alert to every moment and every person. He does not worry about what might happen to him. He walks purposefully in the given hours and shows, by his resurrection and ascension, that there is no barrier between the common and the sacred.

After we sing a hymn, we are released from jail. Rejoicing in the power of the Spirit, we return to the world to tell what we have seen.

. . . . . .